# ACHIEVING ENERGY INDEPENDENCE

A Statement on National Policy by
the Research and Policy Committee
of the Committee
for Economic Development

*December 1974*

**Library of Congress Cataloging in Publication Data**

Committee for Economic Development.
  Achieving energy independence.

  1. Energy policy–United States.   I. Title.
HD9502.U52C65 1974      333.8      74-28488
ISBN  0-87186-057-0 pbk.
ISBN  0-87186-757-5 lib. bdg.

First printing: December 1974
Paperbound: $2.00
Library binding: $3.50
Printed in the United States of America by Georgian Press, Inc.
Design: Harry Carter

COMMITTEE FOR ECONOMIC DEVELOPMENT
477 Madison Avenue, New York, N.Y. 10022

# Contents

RESPONSIBILITY FOR CED STATEMENTS ON NATIONAL POLICY     4

PURPOSE OF THIS STATEMENT     7

ACHIEVING ENERGY INDEPENDENCE     11

1. ENERGY INDEPENDENCE AND HOW TO ATTAIN IT     13

    *Priorities*   15

    *Sources of the Energy Crisis*   19

    *Policy Goals and Means*   22

    *Government and Industry*   24

    *SUMMARY OF RECOMMENDATIONS*   25

2. CONSERVING ENERGY USE:
    FIRST STEP TOWARD INDEPENDENCE     30

    *Restraining Demand*   31

    *Prices and Efficiency*   32

    *Efficiency, Equity, and Inflation*   37

    *Program for More Efficient Energy Use*   38

3. SUPPLY: INDEPENDENCE AND REDUNDANCY     42

    *How Much Is Enough?*   42

    *Near-Term Possibilities: Familiar Fuels*   43

    *Other Available Sources of Energy*   45

    *Reducing Uncertainty*   46

    *Near-Term Trade-offs between the Environment
       and Increased Energy Production*   48

    *Medium-Term Possibilities: Synthetic Fuels
       and Breeder Reactors*   49

    *Long-Term Prospects: Research*   53

    *Capital Costs*   54

    *Reserves and Standby Capacity*   56

4. GOVERNMENT ORGANIZATION FOR ENERGY ADMINISTRATION     57

    *The President and Energy Policy*   58

    *Accelerating Research and Development*   59

    *Energy Regulation*   61

    *Department of Energy and Natural Resources*   62

    *Energy and Mineral Resources Administration*   63

    *Integration of Environmental Protection and
       Resource Development at the Cabinet Level*   64

    *Congressional Organization for Legislative Policy on Energy*   65

MEMORANDA OF COMMENT, RESERVATION, OR DISSENT     69

CED: A BUSINESS-ACADEMIC PARTNERSHIP     93

**Responsibility for CED Statements on National Policy**

The Committee for Economic Development is an independent research and educational organization of two hundred business executives and educators. CED is nonprofit, nonpartisan, and nonpolitical. Its purpose is to propose policies that will help to bring about steady economic growth at high employment and reasonably stable prices, increase productivity and living standards, provide greater and more equal opportunity for every citizen, and improve the quality of life for all. A more complete description of the objectives and organization of CED is to be found in the section "CED: A Business-Academic Partnership."

All CED policy recommendations must have the approval of the Research and Policy Committee, a group of sixty trustees whose names are listed on these pages. This Committee is directed under the bylaws to "initiate studies into the principles of business policy and of public policy which will foster the full contribution by industry and commerce to the attainment and maintenance" of the objectives stated above. The bylaws emphasize that "all research is to be thoroughly objective in character, and the approach in each instance is to be from the standpoint of the general welfare and not from that of any special political or economic group." The Committee is aided by a Research Advisory Board of leading social scientists and by a small permanent professional staff.

The Research and Policy Committee offers this statement as an aid in bringing about greater understanding of actions that should be taken to

4

meet energy needs without compromising basic objectives for the security of the nation and its allies, jeopardizing a sound domestic and international economy, or endangering the environment. The Committee is not attempting to pass judgment on any pending specific legislative proposals; its purpose is to urge careful consideration of the objectives set forth in the statement and of the best means of accomplishing those objectives.

Each statement on national policy is preceded by discussions, meetings, and exchanges of memoranda, often stretching over many months. The research is undertaken by a subcommittee, assisted by advisors chosen for their competence in the field under study. The members and advisors of the Subcommittee on Problems and Potentials of Economic Growth: The Energy Problem, which prepared this statement, are listed on the following page.

The full Research and Policy Committee participates in the drafting of findings and recommendations. Likewise, the trustees on the drafting subcommittee vote to approve or disapprove a policy statement, and they share with the Research and Policy Committee the privilege of submitting individual comments for publication, as noted on this and the following page and on the appropriate page of the text of the statement.

*Except for the members of the Research and Policy Committee and the responsible subcommittee, the recommendations presented herein are not necessarily endorsed by other trustees or by the advisors, contributors, staff members, or others associated with CED.*

# Purpose
# of this Statement

WHEN THE CED RESEARCH AND POLICY COMMITTEE, in the spring of 1973, authorized the studies that led to this statement, the energy situation confronting the United States was serious but not critical. It was a major example of how economic growth was depleting supplies of raw materials. The focus of concern was the increasing dependence of the United States and of other industrial nations on imported oil as a source of energy. The fundamental issue, as this Committee then saw it, was how the nation could best meet its energy needs over the next ten to fifteen years without compromising basic objectives for national security, a sound economy, the balance of payments, and the environment. In more practical terms, we sought answers to these basic questions:

What policies are available to increase domestic supply, and how hard should they be pushed?

What policies are available to slow the increase in energy consumption, and how should they be used?

How can the United States best deal with the problems that arise because the richest supplies of crude oil are found in one part of the world but most of the consumption occurs elsewhere?

7

These fundamental questions remain. But what has changed between then and now (and it is a very big change indeed) is that the time for choosing among the various policy alternatives has run out, just as the number of available choices has been reduced.

**What to do now.** The events of late 1973 and early 1974 (the outbreak of war in the Middle East, the oil embargo by the Arab nations, and the huge boost in world oil prices) have created an urgency that hardly needs emphasizing at this point.

The question is no longer what to do in ten or fifteen years; rather, it is what to do *now* in order to meet the nation's energy needs most effectively without compromising the basic national and international objectives set forth at the outset of this study. We therefore concentrate on the steps that may be taken at once to conserve the use of energy and to establish a set of priorities for increasing production as rapidly as possible without ignoring long-range needs.

This Committee's central concern is that the United States act immediately to minimize its vulnerability to the threat of another oil embargo. The statement outlines what we believe to be a practical program for implementing this vital and awesome commitment.

**International aspects.** Meanwhile, the Committee is making an intensive study of the international economic and financial implications of the current energy crisis. This study grew out of, and builds on, the International Symposium on Energy and Raw Materials in Paris in June 1974. It is being carried forward jointly with our counterpart groups in foreign countries, who, with CED, sponsored the Paris conference. These groups are the German CEPES (European Committee for Economic and Social Progress), the French CRC (Research and Study Center for Business Executives), the British PEP (Political and Economic Planning), CEDA (Committee for Economic Development of Australia), the Swedish SNS (Industrial Council for Social and Economic Studies), and Keizai Doyukai (Japan Committee for Economic Development).

We have held preliminary meetings with these groups and are moving forward with them to early conclusion of the joint study and publication of our common findings.

**Acknowledgments.** The Committee is greatly indebted to the various groups and individuals who made the successful conclusion of our eighteen-month energy project possible. In particular, we appreciate the generosity of the Richard King Mellon Foundation in funding the studies and research leading to this statement. Leadership for the project was provided by William H. Franklin, chairman of Caterpillar Tractor Company, who undertook the arduous assignment of chairing the Subcommittee on Problems and Potentials of Economic Growth: The Energy Problem. Arnold H. Packer, senior economist of CED, was responsible as project director for guiding the research.

Philip M. Klutznick, *Chairman*
*Research and Policy Committee*

# Achieving
# Energy
# Independence

## U.S. ENERGY GAP PROJECTED TO 1985, BASED ON SUPPLY AND DEMAND TRENDS PRIOR TO OIL BOYCOTT

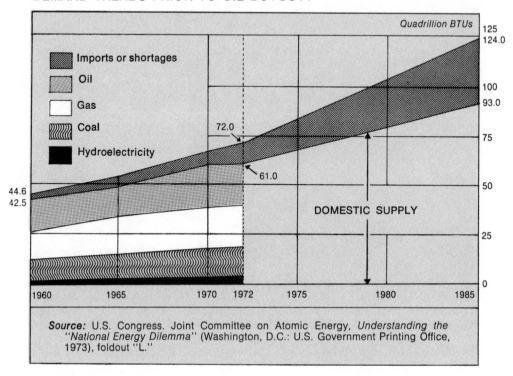

Source: U.S. Congress. Joint Committee on Atomic Energy, *Understanding the "National Energy Dilemma"* (Washington, D.C.: U.S. Government Printing Office, 1973), foldout "L."

**Figure 1.** U.S. self-sufficiency in oil ended by 1970. Although consumption grew less rapidly in the United States than it did in the rest of the world, the nation was already consuming so much that each year's increment was very large. The discovery of new domestic supplies of oil and natural gas barely kept up with the depletion of known reserves. Domestic production leveled off, and by 1968, spare capacity fell below the level of oil imports. By 1973, imports had grown to one-third of U.S. oil consumption, and because consumption was growing more rapidly than production, the nation's dependence on foreign oil continued to increase. Prior to the crisis of October 1973, it was projected that U.S. imports of oil and gas would be 11 million barrels per day by 1980 and 14 million barrels by 1985, or approximately half of U.S. oil consumption. Total energy imports were projected to be one-fourth of total U.S. energy consumption in 1985.

# 1. Energy Independence and How to Attain It

THE ERA OF CHEAP ENERGY has ended abruptly, with serious consequences both for the United States and for the rest of the world. Escalation of energy prices, massive and uncontrolled accumulation of financial assets in the hands of the oil-producing countries, and continuing vulnerability to another oil embargo gravely threaten the economic and political stability of many nations. Strenuous efforts to conserve energy and to expand domestic production are clearly indicated as the basis for prudent national policy. Yet, a year after the embargo, the United States has only begun to get its house in order. It still depends on imports for almost two-fifths of its oil, or the equivalent of about one-sixth of its total energy supply.*

*We believe that the United States must act immediately to minimize its vulnerability to the threat of another oil embargo.* This implies that the United States must be able to forgo the use of most imported oil for an extended period if necessary. Achieving this goal will require changes in the American way of life, but these changes will have to be made if the nation is to protect its political and economic security (see Figure 1).

See memorandum by *JAMES Q. RIORDAN, page 70.

In order to reduce the nation's dependence on imports, it is necessary to reduce the growth of demand (which can be done soon) and to increase supply (which will take longer). In order to import less, the United States will have to devote considerably more of its labor, capital, and intellectual resources to producing energy and less to producing other things. In addition to paying a higher dollar price for energy, this country will have to suspend or defer some environmental improvement and consume considerably less energy than it would if energy were more abundant. Conservation will not take place unless current patterns of energy consumption in industry, transportation, and homes are modified. Changes beyond those induced by higher prices will not be forthcoming unless an enlightened political leadership convinces the public that the benefits of energy independence are worth the effort. Moreover, the energy functions of the executive branch, Congress, and the regulatory agencies of the government will have to be reorganized if an effective policy is to be formulated and implemented.

U.S. energy independence will not, by itself, put an end to the energy problem. The problem will persist for the extended period of European and Japanese energy dependence. However, the commitment to independence will strengthen the United States in its negotiations with the oil-exporting countries and will reassure its allies. Beyond these near-term advantages, a substantial change in U.S. patterns of consumption and production will go a long way toward easing the world's transition to an era in which oil and gas are no longer the major sources of energy.

The purpose of this statement is to suggest what actions the government should take *now* in order to meet the nation's energy needs most effectively without compromising basic objectives for the security of the United States and its allies, jeopardizing a sound domestic and international economy, or endangering the environment.*

A program to achieve independence will have to contain the many elements described in this policy statement. In summary, they include:

Developing practical storage capacity, reserve production capacity, and emergency conservation measures to weather disruption of import supply without undue economic consequences**

Continuing and increasing energy conservation measures that will reduce demand for energy

Stepping up research and development to improve efficiency in energy use

Improving the domestic supply of oil, gas, coal, and uranium and of synthetic oil and gas from oil shale and coal

See memoranda by *ROBERT B. SEMPLE and by FRAZAR B. WILDE, page 71.
See memorandum by **GEORGE C. McGHEE, page 71.

Developing new technology that will provide alternatives for energy production beyond 1990

Making organizational changes in government and in its relationship with industry that are necessary to carry out this Committee's recommendations for bringing energy supply and demand into better balance.*

## Priorities

Policies that can have an early impact by reducing demand or increasing supply should be implemented immediately. At the same time, work will have to begin now on programs requiring long lead time if these are to be ready when needed.

The problem of establishing priorities is complicated by the extraordinary uncertainty of the energy situation. The actions of the Organization of the Petroleum Exporting Countries (OPEC) are no more predictable than success in finding new oil and gas fields.** Nor can technological progress with new forms of energy be made in accordance with a predictable schedule. Plans must remain flexible, and flexibility implies the simultaneous pursuit of many options and hence possible redundancy. Nevertheless, priorities must be set, if on no other basis than the time it will probably take to get things accomplished.

Energy conservation is the quickest and surest path to reduced imports.*** Driving less and at reduced speeds, improving the insulation of buildings, setting thermostats higher in summer and lower in winter, and monitoring industrial energy consumption closely have already had an impact and can make an even greater contribution in the immediate future. The consumption of gasoline and the use of electricity in the third quarter of 1974 was essentially the same as it was in the third quarter of 1973. Energy consumption was about 5 percent less in the summer of 1974 than might have been anticipated a year earlier; significantly, this was after the end of the embargo and its associated fuel shortages. Part of this reduction in demand was undoubtedly a temporary cyclical response to the economic downturn, but much was a more permanent adaptation to higher prices. This recent experience indicates the potential for conservation; policy should be directed to encouraging this trend.

The first priority for energy conservation is the more efficient use of existing homes, appliances, automobiles, and industrial equipment. Over the longer run, as the current stock of buildings, transportation systems,

See memorandum by *PHILIP SPORN, page 72.
See memorandum by **PHILIP SPORN, page 73.
See memorandum by ***E. SHERMAN ADAMS, page 73.

## POSSIBLE PATTERN OF U.S. ENERGY SUPPLY AND DEMAND IN 1985 TO HOLD IMPORTS TO 10 PERCENT OF TOTAL USE (quadrillion BTUs)

|  | 1972 | 1985 |
|---|---|---|
| **DEMAND** | | |
| Residential and commercial[a] | 13.5 | 15.5 |
| Industrial[a] | 17.5 | 23.5 |
| Transportation[a] | 18.0 | 25.0 |
| Electric utilities | 18.5 | 31.0 |
| Nonenergy uses (e.g., plastics) | 4.5 | 8.0 |
| Synthetic fuel production | — | 2.0 |
| TOTAL | 72.0 | 105.0 |
| | | |
| **DOMESTIC PRODUCTION** | | |
| Oil | | |
| Conventional[b] | 23.0 | 28.5 |
| Synthetic | — | 2.0 |
| Gas | | |
| Conventional | 22.5 | 26.5 |
| Synthetic | — | 1.5 |
| Coal[c] | 12.0 | 21.5 |
| Nuclear | 0.5 | 10.0 |
| Hydroelectric, geothermal, solar | 3.0 | 5.0 |
| TOTAL | 61.0 | 95.0 |
| | | |
| **IMPORTS** | | |
| Oil | 10.0 | 8.5 |
| Gas | 1.0 | 1.5 |
| TOTAL | 11.0 | 10.0 |
| | | |
| **TOTAL SUPPLY, DOMESTIC PRODUCTION AND IMPORTS** | 72.0 | 105.0 |

*Note:* One quadrillion British thermal units (BTUs) equals the amount of energy produced by 172 million barrels of oil, 1 trillion cubic feet of natural gas, or 41.6 million tons of coal.
aExcludes electricity.
bIncludes natural gas liquids.
cDirect use plus energy for synthetic fuel production.

*Sources:* Data for 1972: Data Resources Incorporated Energy Databank; U.S. Department of the Interior, Bureau of Mines, March 13, 1974, news release.
Data for 1985: A. H. Packer, S. Park, and W. Flaherty, "The Cost of Self-sufficiency," CED staff paper (available upon request).

16

How Curtailing Imports Could Affect Supply and Demand. An effective national commitment to energy independence will require both an increase in domestic production and restraint on consumption to reduce imports of oil and gas. This Committee proposes that the national goal should be to reduce oil and gas imports to no more than 10 percent of total energy consumption and to limit annual growth in demand to less than 3 percent. The table illustrates one of many possible patterns that might be adopted in order to achieve this goal. The numbers are intended, not as a forecast or a master plan, but as a quantitative description of what is possible if the nation devotes itself to the task.

The 1985 projection shows oil and gas imports to be 10 quads (quadrillion British thermal units), or a little less than 10 percent of total demand. This compares with the 1972 level, when imports supplied 11.0 quads, or 15.3 percent of energy demand. To offset this reduction in foreign supply, domestic energy production would have to be stepped up to an annual rate of increase of 3.4 percent, as compared with an annual growth rate of only 2.6 percent over the period from 1967 to 1972. Coal and nuclear sources now account for slightly more than one-sixth of total energy supply, but they would account for nearly one-third in 1985. Synthetic oil and gas would provide nearly 4 percent of domestic output.

The projection assumes an annual growth rate in energy demand of 2.9 percent during the period from 1972 to 1985, compared with an average growth rate of 4.3 percent from 1967 to 1972. However, this growth rate still permits an increase in per capita energy consumption of almost 2 percent annually, or about one-fourth more than the average for the last twenty-five years (but only two-thirds the rate for the last decade). A slowdown of this magnitude in the growth rate of energy use need not bring about a corresponding reduction in the growth rate of employment or living standards, but the composition of both would have to change.

Limiting imports to 10 percent of energy consumption will achieve the objective of independence only if the country is able to manage without that 10 percent if it becomes necessary. The supply-demand balance shown in the table satisfies this criterion. During an embargo, oil consumption could be cut back by 5 quads, chiefly from the transportation sector, and the additional 5 quads of supply could come from standby arrange-

18

and energy-using devices is replaced, energy efficiency can be built into the economy permanently. *The nation's conservation goal should be to limit the average growth rate of energy consumption to less than 3 percent annually in a high-employment economy.\* Supply must increase more rapidly than demand.* This is the only way in which the United States can reduce the import share of its energy needs and avoid the situation shown in Figure 1.

We do not intend to predict what supply or demand will be in the future, nor do we think it wise for the country to commit itself irrevocably to specific quantitative goals. But we do believe that an irrevocable commitment to independence should be made. *The general objective of U.S. policies should be to reduce oil imports to no more than 10 percent of total energy consumption by 1985 and to be able to withstand any embargo that might occur before then* ( see table on page 16). This is what energy independence means.

Although we are convinced that such a goal is attainable, we are fully aware that only determined and immediate action will bring it to realization in this span of time. It is therefore vitally important to distinguish between short-term, readily accomplished objectives and longer-term, potentially desirable objectives.

Before the middle of the 1980s, substantial increases in domestic supply can be expected only in those fuels and processes already in widespread use: conventional oil, natural gas and coal, and electricity generated from coal and uranium.\*\* The contribution of new processes based on known technologies (such as synthetic oil and gas from oil shale and coal or energy from the next generation of nuclear reactors) will begin to be felt in the mid-1980s only if a crash program is undertaken immediately. Finally, widespread use of solar and geothermal energy is even farther off, and nuclear fusion is unlikely to supply a substantial portion of energy in

---

ments to increase supply and switch fuels. This gives the United States the capacity to forgo imports from even secure sources of supply. If we are to share the shortage with other friendly nations, the capability to do without imports entirely may be necessary in order to make up the loss from the boycotting countries.

---

See memorandum by \*THOMAS G. AYERS, page 74.
See memorandum by \*\*SHEARON HARRIS, page 74.

this century.* Nevertheless, work must begin now if these technologies are to be available at the appropriate time.

Thus, U.S. priorities for increasing supply must be, first, to expand the supply of the familiar fuels; second, to introduce new processes; and third, to develop new technologies.**

Energy policy raises other complicated problems that are not covered in detail in this statement. One issue is the relationship between the investment requirements of the energy industry and the overall capital needs of U.S. industry. A second and related issue is the international economic and financial implications of the high prices of OPEC oil. A third issue is the relationship between energy prices and inflation and the burden that these put on low-income individuals. All three problems are currently under study by other CED subcommittees.

### Sources of the Energy Crisis

The lifting of the oil embargo in March 1974 did not end the energy crisis. The fourfold increase in the price of Middle Eastern crude oil since the summer of 1973 has created another crisis for the United States and other industrial countries and potentially calamitous problems for the poorest countries. Moreover, there is no assurance that supplies will not be interrupted again; the disappearance of waiting lines at gasoline stations is no signal to relax.

Nor did the Arab embargo in the fall of 1973 initiate the energy problem. Even prior to this event, the need to adjust to the growing scarcity of fossil fuels was becoming evident. The prospect of energy scarcity had been obscured during most of the postwar period because discovery of oil, in particular, exceeded consumption. The prodigious discoveries of easily accessible oil in the Middle East and elsewhere made world oil prices cheaper through the 1960s than they were a decade earlier. But the tide began to change in the last few years, at least partially because of the earlier drop in prices. World energy consumption grew at an average annual rate of 5.7 percent during the period from 1967 to 1972, and oil consumption grew even faster, as cheap oil replaced coal in Europe and Japan as well as in the United States. With the evaporation of spare capacity at the end of the decade, U.S. self-sufficiency also ended. The stage was now set for OPEC to exercise effectively the economic and political power afforded by their resources. (See "OPEC Leverage over World Oil Prices," pages 20 and 21.)

See memorandum by *ELVIS J. STAHR, page 74.
See memorandum by **IAN MacGREGOR, page 74.

## OPEC LEVERAGE OVER WORLD OIL PRICES

Two-thirds of the free world's proven reserves of oil are in the Middle East, and 40 percent of that is in Saudi Arabia. Moreover, it costs relatively little to develop and produce oil in that area (only $.20 a barrel in some places). Until 1972, the price of Middle Eastern oil was relatively low; thus, for security reasons, the United States imposed oil-import quotas to maintain a healthy but higher-cost domestic industry in the face of low-priced foreign competition. But the era of low-priced oil was not to endure.

The first augury of change came in the 1960s, when the members of OPEC cooperated successfully in resisting a reduction of posted oil prices and proceeded to increase per-barrel royalty and tax payments. By 1971, this experience encouraged OPEC to determine world oil production and prices unilaterally. It was strengthened in this endeavor by the exhaustion of U.S. spare capacity, which had helped to offset the oil shortage that occurred during the 1967 Arab-Israeli War. The Arab governments used embargoes and production cutbacks to achieve political ends, and the OPEC members' take per barrel rose from less than $1 in 1970 to more than $9 in 1974. This increase and the almost certain dependence of much of the world on Middle Eastern oil for the next fifteen or twenty years created the energy crisis.

The country's new environmental awareness was one reason why the end of U.S. self-sufficiency came when it did. Energy production and use inevitably have environmental consequences. Ten years ago, these consequences were undervalued, and the environment suffered. The strenuous and necessary effort to correct this imbalance, however, cannot ignore the trade-off required: a cleaner environment requires more capital and labor to supply the same amount of useful energy. Normally, higher energy costs would have meant less consumption of the affected fuels. But in the case of oil and gas, environmental protection measures resulted in in-

The benefits of U.S. energy independence must be evaluated in the perspective of an international strategy. In the highly unlikely event that the United States did not import any oil, OPEC exports might be reduced by one-fourth (based on pre-1973 projections). If the price of OPEC oil were responsive to the volume exported, then reducing U.S. imports would reduce world oil prices, which would further moderate the OPEC trade surplus and the world's balance-of-payments problems. However, the price of OPEC oil (especially from the Middle East) bears little relationship to its cost. Substantial quantities of oil can be profitably sold in the United States for $2 a barrel, less than one-fifth of the current price of oil delivered to the East Coast. OPEC could adjust oil production to maintain a target price irrespective of overall demand, as it did in the summer of 1974.

Moreover, the OPEC target price may be governed by the price of domestically produced U.S. oil. The more self-sufficient the United States becomes, the higher the price of domestic oil will be because this will require, for example, more expensive methods to find and produce oil. Thus, if OPEC decides to set its price equal to the U.S. price, a zero-import policy might have the paradoxical result of bringing about higher world oil prices than a U.S. policy of moderate imports would.

Although the price effects of a zero-import policy are ambiguous, the potential dangers of being unable to do without imports are clear. Dependence on uncertain sources for an essential commodity means that there is no way to withstand a sudden increase in price; dependence therefore encourages price increases. This was the experience of 1973.

creased consumption. The shift away from coal that followed the passage of the 1970 amendment to the Clean Air Act and the delay in the introduction of nuclear power meant a shift to oil and natural gas. At least initially, auto-emission-control devices meant less useful energy per gallon of gasoline consumed. Environmental concerns also reduced energy supplies by slowing efforts to drill offshore, to develop the Alaskan oil fields and gas resources, and to construct nuclear power plants.

The simultaneous onset of these three related developments (the end of U.S. self-sufficiency, OPEC cohesiveness, and environmental controls) set the stage for the extraordinarily rapid increase in energy prices. The rapidity of these changes in energy economics means that reestablishing U.S. energy independence will be an expensive undertaking. The cost of independence will be high because the country was unprepared for the events of 1973. The United States did not build stockpiles when oil was inexpensive, nor did it begin to bring supply and demand into balance when there was time to make the transition gradually. With hindsight, it is clear that this country's capability to forgo uncertain foreign supplies should have been continuously maintained.

## Policy Goals and Means

The energy crisis has four separate dimensions for the United States: first, the threat to U.S. foreign policy and military security arising from a potential embargo;* second, the threat of continued worldwide inflation arising from a potential further escalation of energy prices; third, the threat to the stability of the international financial system arising from the payments imbalance between OPEC and the oil-importing countries; and fourth, the threat of recession following from the readjustment required by the energy shortage and the first three factors.

The United States cannot solve any of these problems by itself. We believe the United States should take an international stance on energy questions that is consistent with its leadership role in world affairs. Although current U.S. dependence on uncertain foreign energy sources cannot be allowed to persist in the hope that the events of 1973 and 1974 will not be repeated, neither can the United States withdraw completely from world trade in energy. Even if the United States could become self-sufficient in oil, it would need to import other essential goods and to facilitate payments by other oil importers through trade with them. More importantly, the world's peace and security cannot be ensured by U.S. self-sufficiency alone.

Achieving independence will not free this nation from OPEC pressures that could potentially be applied to other oil-importing countries. Although energy independence would undoubtedly lessen U.S. vulnerability to political blackmail, the capacity to shut down Europe and Japan would still be a powerful weapon in the hands of the oil-exporting nations. If this country agrees to share energy shortages with its allies, as we believe it should, U.S. policies will have to reflect the continuing dependence of the rest of the industrial world on OPEC oil. The United States

See memorandum by *PHILIP SPORN, page 75.

should also recognize that an international commitment to share the shortage would make it more difficult for producers to threaten or to impose an embargo.*

We endorse the steps taken by the twelve-nation energy coordinating group toward the development of an integrated emergency program to reduce consumption and share supplies if an embargo occurs. We would also welcome other multinational actions such as joint research and development programs. We recognize the risks associated with such a cooperative response. A common policy means *sharing the shortage* if an embargo occurs. Cooperation means finding a compromise satisfactory to high-import countries (such as Japan), which import all their oil and use much of it for industrial purposes, and high-consumption countries (such as the United States), which have substantial domestic resources. An international stance also implies avoiding exclusive bilateral arrangements between consuming countries and producing countries.

The current oil situation threatens to destabilize the U.S. balance-of-payments structure and the exchange rate of the U.S. dollar. This problem, like the security problem, will not be eliminated by U.S. self-sufficiency. An imbalance in the international flow of goods and financial resources is likely as long as the members of OPEC run massive current account surpluses with the rest of the world. It will inevitably require that the United States tolerate substantial current account deficits. The U.S. deficit will not be determined solely by its own oil imports or trade deficit with OPEC and is likely to be influenced more by the investment choices of the members of OPEC and the financial arrangements made to "recycle" these funds.†**

The most important determinants of the U.S. deficit on current account are likely to be world oil prices and the total quantity of oil imported; more precisely, it is the money collected by OPEC members beyond their capacity to spend it. *Therefore, an important objective of U.S. energy policy should be to moderate world oil prices and demand.* The development of conservation techniques and of alternative energy resources (such as solar and nuclear energy) that can be used throughout the world may be more important to U.S. payments balances than development of resources that reduce U.S. dependency only.***

---

†This policy statement will not deal with those recycling arrangements. However, the subject is under intensive study by another CED subcommittee in cooperation with CED counterpart organizations in six other countries.

See memorandum by *FRAZAR B. WILDE, page 76.
See memorandum by **FRAZAR B. WILDE, page 76.
See memoranda by ***PHILIP SPORN and by ELVIS J. STAHR, page 76.

Energy independence will moderate but not eliminate either the risk of political blackmail or the balance-of-payments problem. Independence is worth the cost because it will give the United States and its allies more options and will thereby place a limit on the political and economic price that the oil-exporting countries can charge for their product.

A basic element of U.S. energy strategy must be flexibility. The winter of 1973–1974 was especially difficult because options were not available. Substantial economic dislocation was the only alternative to importing oil. A policy of independence would enable the United States to respond flexibly to changes in world oil prices and availability.

Forgoing imports entirely would be a mistake unless domestic fuels were less expensive. The additional capital investment required to attain complete self-sufficiency would be extremely large. Furthermore, substantial imports are available from sources not likely to join in an embargo; and even if these imports had to be shared during an embargo, there are ways to mitigate the effects of a considerable reduction in oil imports. Moreover, the combination of U.S. flexibility and a tolerable level of imports might encourage some oil-producing countries to lower their prices. In contrast, a policy of eliminating imports would mean that the lure of selling additional quantities (the usual incentive for price reductions) would not apply to the oil-exporting countries.

### Government and Industry

The first policy question is the choice of goals; the second is the selection of means. We believe that ending this country's dependence on imported oil requires a new partnership between government and industry. Such a relationship must preserve the efficiencies of private enterprise and the market-price system while recognizing government responsibility for national security, equity, and environmental protection and for aiding overall economic growth.*

Although we prefer the marketplace to the government in directing scarce resources to their most efficient use, unguided economic forces alone cannot be allowed to determine the production, consumption, and price of energy. Some government guidance is necessary if only because adequate and reliable energy supplies are required for the maintenance of economic and military security, both domestically and internationally.

We believe that selective regulations or incentives will have to be employed to complement market forces. Increased reliance on higher

See memorandum by *PHILIP SPORN, page 77.

prices to reduce demand and to improve efficiency of allocation raises important questions of equity, especially because it raises producers' profits and imposes new burdens on those consumers and businesses least able to bear them. The government will have to consider measures to help those who are most damaged cope with higher energy prices.

Government guidance is best provided in the American system by establishing an understandable set of rules and incentives within which the private sector can operate. In general, exploration, development, and allocation of energy among alternative uses will be determined most efficiently if consumers and producers can respond to relative prices and profit opportunities. Government policy should ensure that its own actions do not prevent these signals from working and that the prices and profit opportunities lead to responses that satisfy national goals.

# Summary
# of Recommendations

A broad range of actions will be needed to moderate demand and increase domestic energy production, including many changes at the federal, state, and local levels, if a coordinated policy is to be successfully and rapidly implemented.

Policy will have to be flexible and adapt to the unfolding of events both within the United States and internationally. Some of our recommendations for conserving energy will have an immediate effect on the quantity of imports; many of those dealing with supply will not begin to pay off until the end of the decade; still others concerning research and development will not significantly influence U.S. import demand until the end of the century. What is important is that the United States now demonstrate its dedication to energy independence and its resolve to persist in these efforts until full independence is achieved.*

**We recommend that the government develop standby emergency plans, including rationing if necessary, to curtail demand in the event of another embargo or to meet other possible emergencies. Also included in this plan should be a workable mix of a practical petroleum storage system, emergency fuel switching, and emergency oil production.** It will be necessary to modify these plans periodically as the United States makes progress toward its goal of energy independence.***

See memorandum by *JOHN D. GRAY (Omark Industries), page 77.
See memorandum by **GEORGE C. McGHEE, page 71.
See memorandum by ***PHILIP SPORN, page 77.

Restructuring Government Energy Functions. If effective national policy is to lead to energy independence in the near future, the federal government's energy programs, now scattered and diffused, must be entirely reshaped. This process has begun with the passage of the Energy Reorganization Act of 1974, creating the new Energy Resources Council (ERC), Energy Research and Development Administration (ERDA), and Nuclear Regulatory Commission (NRC). In our view, the most urgent requirement now is to establish a cabinet-level organization providing comprehensive overview and administration of the government's energy functions. **We urge that the President and Congress move as rapidly as possible to create a department of energy and natural resources in order to achieve an integrated structure for energy administration in the federal government, which is essential to achieving energy independence.** *

Among the major components to be incorporated into this department would be the Federal Energy Administration (FEA), acting as the department's central planning and directing unit, and, ultimately, the newly formed ERDA. Furthermore, to balance resource use with environmental-quality objectives, we recommend that the Environmental Protection Agency (EPA) be transferred to the department of energy and natural resources as a distinct and major entity of the proposed department. We believe that EPA should be coordinate with, not subordinate to, the energy and mineral resources administration and should be given status and influence commensurate with its important mission. ** We also recommend that the Council on Environmental Quality (CEQ) be retained in the Executive Office of the President as an independent monitor of environmental impact, serving as an advisor to the President, but without regulatory or operational responsibilities. ***

There is also urgent need to modernize the structures of Congress so that it can deal more speedily and effectively with energy legislation. To this end, we suggest changes to unify committee functions in both the House and the Senate and to establish a joint energy and environment committee.

Restraining Demand. **** The government must now be prepared to do more to encourage conservation when normal market forces act too slowly and to moderate the impact of energy scarcity on society. Consumers must be aware of the costs they are incurring; otherwise, higher prices will not bring about reduction in energy use. **We recommend that appliances be clearly labeled to show how much energy they consume.**

See memoranda by *JOHN B. CAVE, by FRANKLIN A. LINDSAY, and by PHILIP SPORN, pages 78 and 79.
See memorandum by **JOHN R. COLEMAN, page 79.
See memorandum by ***ELVIS J. STAHR, page 79.
See memoranda by ****JOSEPH L. BLOCK, by JOHN R. COLEMAN, by LINCOLN GORDON, and by ROBERT R. NATHAN, pages 79, 80, and 81.

Furthermore, new multifamily residential units should contain individual meters for utilities where this is practical. Regulatory authorities should also encourage utilities to install individual meters in existing multifamily structures. Consideration should also be given to establishing penalty rates for energy consumption in excess of some reasonable standard.\* Special efforts should be made to promote the recycling of energy-intensive materials where this is practical and economic. We also recommend a review of rate structures for electricity and natural gas to ensure that price differences reflect cost differences and do not encourage inefficient energy use.\*\* Additionally, we believe that, where necessary, revisions should be made in building codes and Federal Housing Administration regulations in order to encourage use of adequate insulation and other desirable improvements in new structures.

We recommend various conservation measures in the transportation field. To encourage a switch in demand from automobiles to a means of transportation that provides more passenger miles per gallon, we recommend that communities act to improve traffic patterns for buses, taxis, car pools, and other energy-efficient forms of transportation. Similarly, the regulation of freight transport should aim for more ton-miles per unit of energy. In addition, there are opportunities to save energy by getting more miles per gallon out of each automobile or other vehicle. We recommend that a consistent national policy be developed to apply a higher tax to higher-fuel-consumption motor vehicles.\*\*\* Finally, some worthwhile environmental goals may have to be postponed, and some loosening of environmental standards will be necessary until a better energy balance is achieved. We recommend that standards of engine design and automobile-emission control be reviewed with the intent of finding a way to achieve environmental goals with maximum increases in efficiency. We recommend that a highway speed limit (currently 55 miles per hour), resulting in high fuel economy, be retained and enforced.\*\*\*\*

Because regulated prices of natural gas were set too low, the production of gas was inadequate, its allocation between industrial and residential uses was inefficient, and users were encouraged to consume wastefully. We recommend that, except for existing contracts, the wellhead price of natural gas be deregulated and that the demand-reducing effects of higher prices be allowed to function. The tax treatment of any "windfall profits on old gas" should be similar to that recommended later for old oil.†\*\*\*\*\*

---

†See page 47.

See memoranda by \*THOMAS G. AYERS and by PHILIP SPORN, page 82.
See memorandum by \*\*ROBERT D. LILLEY, page 83.
See memoranda by \*\*\*OSCAR A. LUNDIN and by ROBERT B. SEMPLE, pages 83 and 84.
See memorandum by \*\*\*\*ELVIS J. STAHR, page 84.
See memoranda by \*\*\*\*\*THOMAS G. AYERS, by JOSEPH L. BLOCK, by JAMES R. KENNEDY, and by ROBERT B. SEMPLE, pages 84 and 85.

Special measures to alleviate the impact of higher energy prices on particular groups may be desirable not merely on grounds of equity but also as a means of reducing the risk that higher energy prices will serve as a trigger for a continuing wage-price spiral. Various approaches have been proposed to deal with this problem, including selective adjustments in the personal tax structure and selective subsidies. Selective subsidies should be provided for energy-saving activities both to hasten the transition to a more energy efficient economy and to ease the burden for those who cannot afford or adjust to higher energy prices. **We recommend a substantial increase in subsidies for public transportation. The allocation between capital and operating subsidies should be decided by communities on the basis of their specific circumstances.**

Increasing Production.* We believe that doing too much to achieve energy independence is a more acceptable risk than doing too little. Although priorities must be established on the basis of the time required to bring new supplies into use, many alternatives should be pursued. Implementation of this strategy may require that the government assume some of the risks, especially for higher-risk, long-term investments that are vulnerable to a sharp reduction in world oil prices.

**As a matter of foresight and prudence, we believe that the President should have clear authority to establish a system of priorities and allocation governing critical materials and equipment required for energy production upon declaration of a national emergency caused by acute supply shortages that seriously impair U.S. energy independence objectives.**

A primary goal of government policy should be to reduce the uncertainty that now impedes fuel production. **To reduce uncertainty, we recommend leaving the price of newly discovered oil and natural gas uncontrolled; establishing more efficient environmental controls; streamlining procedures for leasing federal oil, coal, shale, and natural gas resources and for siting energy facilities; and leasing environmentally acceptable sites for extraction of oil, gas, coal, and oil shale as rapidly as exploitation can be undertaken.** **

Price controls on old oil (60 percent of domestic production) tend to limit recovery, require a complex government allocation system, and inhibit the demand-suppressing effect of higher prices. Decontrol of old oil prices is therefore directly analogous to the decontrol of natural gas prices. **We recommend phased removal of price controls on old oil, but we recognize that political and social considerations may well require that** "windfall profits on old oil" be taxed unless channeled into net additions to energy-producing investment dedicated to increasing supplies.*

Another major set of uncertainties are those associated with the technologies for synthetic fuels and nuclear fission. **We recommend that to the extent necessary the government fund research, development, and demonstration pilot plants for synthetic fuels from oil shale and coal and also for breeder reactors and other advanced nuclear technologies. In addition, the government should support similar activities for advanced coal mining techniques and related land reclamation and for improved methods of removing sulfur from coal.**

The development of synthetic fuels may require that the federal government take measures to offset market uncertainties caused by OPEC actions. Development may proceed more rapidly if the government eliminates the risk that the possibility of lower OPEC prices poses to private investors. **If private commitments to build adequate synthetic fuel facilities are not made very soon, the government should encourage investment by contracting to buy a substantial quantity of synthetic fuels.** Such take-or-pay contracts would establish a minimum guaranteed price for the synthetic fuels produced by these plants.

Most energy exploitation is capital-intensive. Both long lead times and massive amounts of capital will be involved in the process of achieving energy independence. Oil, gas, and shale leasing is an area in which government action can properly reduce financial requirements and at the same time eliminate some unnecessary uncertainty. The large amount of front-end money now required increases the industry's financial needs and inhibits risk taking. **We recommend that the front-end costs of oil and gas leases be reduced in return for an appropriately designed formula for higher payments on the oil and gas extracted from successfully developed leases.****

Finally, substantial government involvement is justified for those energy sources that are unlikely to be important for ten years or more and that require considerable basic research. **The federal government should fund a substantial basic and applied research program in solar, geothermal, and fusion energy; in more efficient electric power generation; and in innovative techniques such as the use of solid waste as an energy source.*** Whenever possible, these efforts should be internationally coordinated, and the costs should be shared by participating nations.******

See memoranda by *THOMAS G. AYERS, by JOSEPH L. BLOCK, by JAMES R. KENNEDY, and by GEORGE C. McGHEE, pages 84 and 87.

See memorandum by **IAN MacGREGOR, page 87.

See memorandum by ***ELVIS J. STAHR, page 87.

See memoranda by ****PHILIP SPORN and by ELVIS J. STAHR, page 88.

# 2. Conserving Energy Use: First Step Toward Independence

HOLDING DOWN THE CONSUMPTION of energy must be a key element in a national energy policy designed to meet the extraordinary situation that confronts the United States. Opportunities to improve efficiency of energy use should be exploited now and should receive as much attention as opportunities to increase supply. *Conservation should be a full partner in a strategy for bringing supply and demand into better balance.* *

Federal policies should facilitate improvements in the efficiency, production, and use of energy in all sectors of the economy. The government has a number of instruments available for achieving this objective or for otherwise slowing the growth of energy demand. In selecting which measures to use or introduce, the nation must be careful not only to distinguish between short- and long-range impacts but also to weigh the burden of sacrifice and to consider on whom it will fall.

In the present emergency, national energy policy has relied primarily on higher prices as the means of restraining demand. Higher prices have already had an impact on energy consumption in the United States and in other countries. Instead of growing by 5 percent, world oil consumption was less in the first three-quarters of 1974 than it was a year earlier. (One result of this reduction was a temporary oversupply of oil, and OPEC had

30                      See memorandum by *JOSEPH L. BLOCK, page 79.

to reduce production in order to maintain current prices.) In part, this reduced demand reflects the worldwide slowdown in economic activity. But it also reflects improvements in efficiency that were induced by higher prices, and many of these will be retained as economic activity recovers.

Heightened public consciousness of the need for conservation has been another factor in reducing demand, and if this consciousness can be further heightened, conservation can be stepped up. Elimination of the lines at gasoline stations had the unfortunate effect of encouraging the public belief that the energy crisis has subsided, but, in fact, the crisis continues. A public information program urging voluntary energy-conservation measures, as proposed by the administration, is essential in any national energy program.

### Restraining Demand

The government has already intervened and must now be prepared to do more to encourage conservation when normal market forces act too slowly and to moderate the impact of energy scarcity on society. The government can apply various carrot-and-stick techniques. It can restrain energy use by taxing consumption, which would have the effect of further price increases, and at the same time employ subsidies to lower the relative prices of energy-saving devices or materials. Existing regulatory bodies, such as the Federal Power Commission (FPC), can regulate energy use indirectly.

In addition to the use of such powers, it may be necessary for the government to regulate energy directly in extreme cases by allocating fuels or rationing final use. The United States is now importing about two-fifths of its oil, or more than one-sixth of its energy; oil from the boycotting countries represents more than 10 percent of oil imports. As we have stated, this nation should be prepared to do without oil from these countries and without a substantial portion of imports from other countries as well. The government should be in a position to reduce demand, by rationing if necessary, in an efficient and equitable fashion. (The long lines at the gasoline stations in February 1974 did not satisfy this criterion.)

**We recommend that the government develop standby emergency plans, including rationing if necessary, to curtail demand in the event of another embargo or to meet other possible emergencies. Also included in this plan should be a workable mix of a practical petroleum storage system, emergency fuel switching, and emergency oil production. These**

plans should be modified as progress is made toward independence.*

One simple and effective means of curtailing energy consumption emerged from the fuel crisis during the winter of 1973–1974, namely, the reduction of speed limits for motor vehicles. The Committee is impressed by the energy savings that resulted; even more important was the decrease in accident fatalities that accompanied these measures. **We recommend that a highway speed limit (currently 55 miles per hour), resulting in high fuel economy, be retained and enforced.**

The habits that Americans developed during the era of cheap energy leave considerable room for improvement. Goods can be produced, homes and offices can be kept comfortable, and people and products can be transported on less energy per unit of service than is now used. Significant improvement can be achieved very quickly if conservation receives the priority it deserves. Moreover, if the transition can be made smoothly and extended over a sufficient span of time, a more moderate rate of growth in energy consumption need not result in increased unemployment, although it may slow growth in productivity and in real GNP (see "Total Energy Consumption and GNP," pages 35 and 36).

### Prices and Efficiency

Energy use in this country has been inefficient because prices have not covered all costs. Although energy prices to individuals have increased substantially, the cost to the country of dependence on foreign energy sources has increased even more and is not fully reflected in prices. Furthermore, the American transportation system was built on a gasoline price that included neither the environmental costs of oil nor the cost of providing the standby arrangements that would have prevented the current problems. Similarly, at least until 1970, the price of coal did not include the environmental cost of its use. Therefore, electricity was to some extent underpriced.

Natural gas provides a painful but graphic illustration of what can happen when an artificially low price is assigned to a resource. Because it is uneconomic to have more than a single pipeline between any two points, the pipeline from the gas fields to the consumption areas is a natural monopoly. Therefore, regulation of the interstate transport of natural gas is necessary. But, there is no reason why competitive market forces cannot operate at the wellhead; many firms can and do sell gas to the pipeline company to be transported. Despite this difference in market structure, FPC began to control the wellhead price of natural gas in 1954.

The wellhead price of natural gas sold in interstate markets was generally constant during the 1960s (about $.15 per thousand cubic feet). In a period when the prices of other goods were rising, this meant that the relative price of natural gas was falling. Production of natural gas rose less than 5 percent between 1970 and 1973; consequently, some new consumers who wanted to buy natural gas at the going price were unable to obtain gas service. Moreover, if it were not for the fact that natural gas is often found during exploration for oil, even less natural gas would have been produced.

In 1973, the controlled price of gas at the wellhead was still less than $.25 per thousand cubic feet, which is equal to $1.50 for the energy contained in a barrel of crude oil. It was sold to New England homeowners for $1.25 per thousand cubic feet, which is equal to $.18 for the energy contained in a gallon of heating oil. Because it is easily transported and clean to burn, natural gas was preferred by industry over other fuels, even at substantially higher prices. Some firms moved to gas-producing states in order to have access to the uncontrolled intrastate market; they were able to bid natural gas away from the controlled interstate market. Thus, despite the fact that the optimum use of natural gas is for home heating, industry was directly consuming over 40 percent of the natural gas produced in the United States, and an additional 16 percent was being used to produce electricity.

Because the price of natural gas was kept below the level that would have balanced supply and demand, some form of rationing had to be used to distribute the natural gas that was available. The implicit rationing mechanism was the denial of gas service to potential new customers. Rationing in this form is not only unfair to those denied service but also leads to inefficient use of scarce resources.

Because regulated prices of natural gas were set too low, the production of gas was inadequate, its allocation between industrial and residential uses was inefficient, and users were encouraged to consume wastefully.

**We recommend that, except for existing contracts, the wellhead price of natural gas be deregulated and that the demand-reducing effects of higher prices be allowed to function.** The tax treatment of any "windfall profits on old gas" should be similar to that recommended later for old oil.[†*]

---

†See page 47.

See memoranda by *THOMAS G. AYERS, by JOSEPH L. BLOCK, by JAMES R. KENNEDY, and by ROBERT B. SEMPLE, pages 84 and 85.

Figure 2. ENERGY USE AT DIFFERENT LEVELS OF GROSS
DOMESTIC PRODUCT, PER CAPITA, SELECTED COUNTRIES, 1970

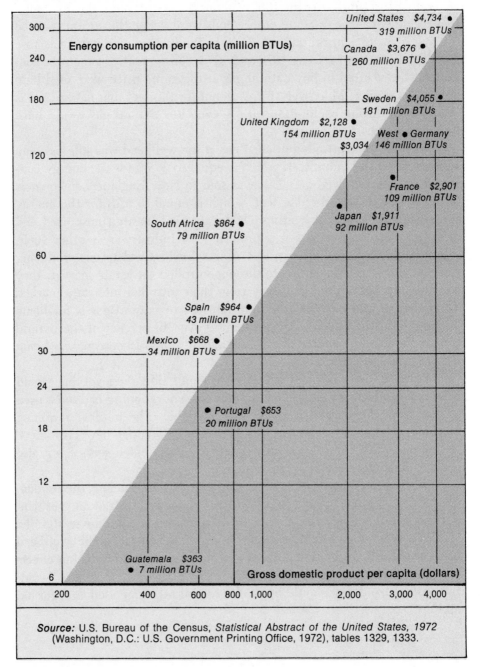

*Source:* U.S. Bureau of the Census, *Statistical Abstract of the United States, 1972* (Washington, D.C.: U.S. Government Printing Office, 1972), tables 1329, 1333.

## Figure 3. RELATIVE ENERGY PRICES (1967 = 1.0)

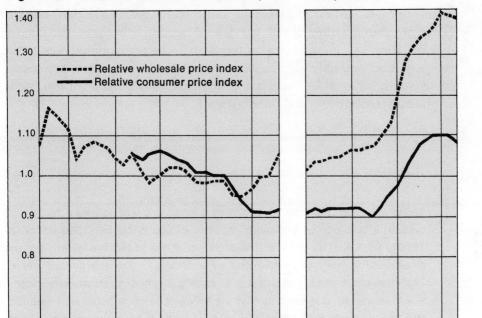

*Sources:* Ratio of wholesale price index for fuel and utilities to wholesale price index for all industrials: Bureau of Labor Statistics; Data Resources Incorporated.

Ratio of composite consumer price index for selected energy items to overall consumer price index: Bureau of Labor Statistics (unpublished series); Data Resources Incorporated.

Total Energy Consumption and GNP. **Higher** living standards have usually been associated with higher per capita energy use (illustrated in Figure 2). But this ratio is not constant and can be changed by events or policy. Canada, for example, uses more energy per dollar of GDP than the simple trend line suggests. Canada's industrial structure and cold climate raise demand at the same time that its ample resources increase supply; a balance is struck at a relatively high quantity of energy per unit of output. Agricultural Guatemala demonstrates the opposite situation.

Figure 3 shows the trend of relative energy prices in the United States over the past two decades. The period from the early 1950s to the mid-

Price decontrol and other government policies should stimulate the search for new natural gas reserves and discourage excess consumption. Complete deregulation of all gas would accomplish these ends most quickly. However, if long-term contracts are to be renegotiated, equitable compensation probably should be provided to the ultimate purchasers. Moreover, it will still be necessary to regulate monopoly situations, such as pipeline transmission and distribution.

---

1960s was characterized by declining prices; this was followed by an increase in U.S. energy consumption from 87,000 BTUs per 1958 dollar in 1966 to 93,000 BTUs in 1972. The substantial rise in relative energy prices since 1972 is likely to be followed by a decline in the energy-GNP ratio. The increase in energy prices has already given energy consumers incentive to conserve. It is obvious that the efficient balance between insulation and use of energy for heating and cooling depends on the relative prices of insulation and energy. The same is true of the trade-off between automobile performance or styling and gasoline economy or between investment in energy-saving equipment and industrial use of energy. Further changes in consumer behavior can be expected, especially in view of the heightened national consciousness of energy shortages.

Current energy consumption patterns provide considerable flexibility for further conservation without significantly reducing standards of living. In 1973, per capita consumption of oil was 1 barrel (42 gallons) every twelve days, although oil provided only 45 percent of total U.S. energy consumption. Total per capita energy consumption is approximately three times greater in the United States than it is in Europe or Japan.

Between 1960 and 1970, per capita energy consumption increased by 33 percent for transportation and by 30 percent for commercial and residential use. These rates of increase need not and should not continue. The shift in demand to smaller automobiles that took place in early 1974 demonstrated the responsiveness of the American consumer to shortages and rapid changes in relative prices. It also demonstrated the great difficulties caused by an abrupt change in consumption patterns.

### Efficiency, Equity, and Inflation

There are several basic criteria to follow in making a choice among instruments for restraining energy demand.

First, the means must be efficient and must make the transition as smooth as possible. Efficiency requires that energy suppliers and users receive price signals that reflect the constantly changing and unpredictable energy situation. The abrupt shifts in 1974 caused by the oil embargo of October 1973 were plainly inefficient. There was no time, for example, to change automobile-production capacity to conform to the new demand pattern. Thus, men became unemployed, and equipment was underutilized.

Second, equity must not be sacrificed. This criterion is more difficult to satisfy because rising energy prices put particular pressure on the budgets of the poor. When this occurs as oil company profits rise, it is not surprising to hear a call for excess profits taxes and price rollbacks. Of course, investors will not put resources into energy-producing industries unless a competitive profit can be made, nor will many consumers reduce their energy consumption unless they feel the pinch of higher prices. Nevertheless, policies aimed at efficiency may not be adopted unless they are perceived as equitable.

In many cases, implicit or explicit contracts have been made on the basis of low energy prices. Communities and other customers have made long-term contracts with pipeline companies for low-priced gas. Consumers have purchased homes with heating-cooling systems and heat-saving characteristics (e.g., insulation) on the assumption that regulated energy prices would not be allowed to increase rapidly. Consumers who have purchased automobiles that consume a gallon or more of gasoline for every ten miles traveled may now wish they had made a different investment. Many have no choice but to commute long distances to work by auto. Similarly, firms that acquired equipment or built factories on the basis of continuing relative declines in energy prices may find themselves at a disadvantage.

Does society have an obligation to protect those who have been hurt by the crisis in energy prices and availability? How can efficiency, which requires higher energy prices as an incentive to conservation, be reconciled with definitions of equity that insist on protecting individuals from these price incentives?

Reconciling efficiency and equity will be considerably less difficult if the principle of compensation is employed. Those receiving social security and welfare payments are compensated through payments adjustments that allow for increases in the consumer price index which occur as energy prices rise. Those who cannot avoid consuming considerable energy may not be fully compensated; however, families who can shift their expenditure patterns to consume less energy may be overcompensated.

Subsidizing public transportation can partially compensate for rising gasoline prices. Because the compensation that subsidies provide is hardly likely to be complete, additional measures may have to be considered in order to mitigate the impact of higher energy prices on persons for whom these price increases impose a disproportionately heavy burden. These measures should seek to provide some degree of equity while reinforcing the incentives for conservation.

Third, different approaches are likely to have different effects on the overall inflationary process. To the extent that the measures adopted result in very large and sudden increases in energy prices, they may serve as a trigger for sharply accelerated wage demands and for other upward ratchet effects on the general price structure, thus contributing to a continuing wage-price spiral. Measures designed to offset inequities created by higher energy prices should also help reduce the extent to which such price increases add to general wage-price pressures.

*We believe that selective subsidies should be provided for energy-saving activities both to hasten the transition to a more energy efficient economy and to ease the burden for those who cannot afford or adjust to higher energy prices.* Although subsidies will change the prices and incentives that a free market might produce, consumers will still be free to choose; there will be no direct government regulation of their individual decisions.*

## Program for More Efficient Energy Use

Our recommendations for increasing energy efficiency cover the three energy-consuming sectors: industrial, residential and commercial, and transportation.** Inevitably, there will be overlaps. One of the government activities that applies to all three sectors is research and development. **We recommend that a significant component of overall funds for energy research and development be used to find ways of improving the efficiency of energy consumption.** In particular, efforts should be directed to the thermal characteristics of buildings and the efficiency of transportation and other energy-using equipment.

See memorandum by *ROBERT D. LILLEY, page 88.
See memorandum by **ROBERT D. LILLEY, page 89.

Industrial. We believe that because of the profit motive, industry will be generally alert to energy-saving opportunities that reduce costs. In order to accelerate industry's response, some means should be developed to share detailed technical information on significant energy-saving projects or techniques. **Special efforts should be made to promote the recycling of energy-intensive materials where this is practical and economic. We also recommend a review of rate structures for electricity and natural gas to ensure that price differences reflect cost differences and do not encourage inefficient energy use.** \* Under the current rate structure, the price of electricity and gas falls with the volume of energy purchased. Although it is appropriate that rates reflect the fixed cost of bringing service to a residence or a business establishment, there are some cases where the rate has been structured to promote additional energy usage. The price of energy must reflect its full current cost to all users if efficiency is to be achieved.

Residential and Commercial. The same observation applies to the residential and commercial sector of the economy. Consumers must be aware of the energy costs they are incurring and must benefit directly from their efforts to conserve; otherwise, higher prices will not bring about the desired reduction in energy use. These conditions do not apply when appliances are unlabeled or when electricity and other utilities are not individually metered, a frequent situation in apartment buildings and offices. **We recommend that appliances be clearly labeled to show how much energy they consume. Furthermore, new multifamily residential units should contain individual meters for utilities where this is practical. Regulatory authorities should also encourage utilities to install individual meters in existing multifamily structures.** Consideration should also be given to establishing penalty rates for energy consumption in excess of some reasonable standard.\*\*

There are other opportunities for making energy use more efficient in the residential and commercial sector. Speculative construction sometimes sacrifices operating costs, including those for energy, in order to minimize the initial purchase price. Homes are often inadequately insulated, and office space frequently requires year-round air conditioning because no provision has been made to open windows or otherwise take advantage of cooler outside temperatures. In general, higher energy prices will bring about more investment in energy conservation. However, in some cases, exploiting the opportunities to increase efficiency will require or will benefit from government action. **We recommend**

See memorandum by \*ROBERT D. LILLEY, page 83.
See memoranda by \*\*THOMAS G. AYERS and by PHILIP SPORN, page 82.

revising building codes and Federal Housing Administration regulations where necessary to encourage use of adequate insulation and other desirable improvements in new structures. Effective insulation standards should be formulated by an agency such as the Bureau of Standards. It may also be desirable to provide limited tax credits to homeowners who insulate their homes.

Transportation. U.S. energy independence requires conservation in the transportation sector. Well over half of the petroleum used in this country provides transportation services. Fortunately, there are numerous opportunities for savings, especially if government policy reinforces the efficiency incentives provided by higher fuel prices.

Moderately priced, convenient public transportation that gives the commuter an alternative to his private automobile can both reduce gasoline demand and lessen the burden of higher energy prices on those people with low and middle incomes. These systems require federal aid. In the past, federal subsidies have been limited to capital equipment because of the potential abuse of operating subsidies. But, some studies show that this restriction has led to excessive investment in equipment and a corresponding lack of attention to maintenance. It is important that careful attention be given to designing an efficient subsidy program. **We recommend a substantial increase in subsidies for public transportation. The allocation between capital and operating subsidies should be decided by communities on the basis of their specific circumstances.**

Public transportation is intended primarily to switch demand from automobiles to a form of transportation that provides more passenger miles per energy unit. With this objective in mind, **we recommend that communities act to improve traffic patterns for buses, taxis, car pools, and other energy-efficient forms of transportation.** In some cases, this may require restricting auto and truck access to portions of the central city at certain times of day. Both these restrictions and public transportation subsidies should be made with the recognition that the public as a whole suffers in a number of ways as a result of traffic congestion.

Similarly, the regulation of freight transport should aim for more ton-miles per unit of energy. **We recommend that Interstate Commerce Commission regulations be modified to encourage fuel efficiency.** Current ICC regulations are often directed toward avoiding excessive competition in the transportation industry. At times, pursuit of this objective has led to energy-wasting practices. For example, the value-of-service rate structure enforced by ICC frequently prevents railroads from reducing their price for transporting high-value manufactured goods. As a result, these goods are shipped by truck, which is more convenient but also more energy intensive. Moreover, the service that individual trucking firms may offer between various locations is regulated in a way that sometimes leads to situations in which trucks must return empty from their initial destination. The Civil Aeronautics Board should also seek to improve energy efficiency in the exercise of its regulatory powers. Its objectives should include maintaining and, if possible, increasing the recent improvement in the ratio of filled to empty seats on a typical flight.

In addition to switching to more efficient forms of transportation, there are opportunities to save energy by getting more miles per gallon out of each automobile or other vehicle. High-horsepower automobiles add disproportionately to energy and transportation problems. Their presence adversely affects the safety of smaller, more energy efficient autos. In some states and localities, this burden is reflected in auto fees and taxes that are based on vehicle weight and horsepower. **We recommend that a consistent national policy be developed to apply a higher tax to higher-fuel-consumption motor vehicles.**\*

Finally, some worthwhile environmental goals may have to be postponed until a better energy balance is achieved. Some loosening of environmental standards will be necessary if the nation's coal resources are to be fully utilized. This may be only a temporary postponement until efficient stack scrubbers are available. Technological advances may also improve the trade-off between the environment and gasoline efficiency. **We recommend that standards of engine design and automobile-emission control be reviewed with the intent of finding a way to achieve environmental goals with maximum increases in efficiency.**

In the policy statement *More Effective Programs for a Cleaner Environment* (1974), we recognized the usefulness of experiments that would substitute effluent fees for regulation as a means of limiting water pollution. We noted that the same general principles should apply to sulfur emissions and air pollution. Such fees avoid arbitrary government decisions about technological feasibility. They also tend to establish a balance between the social cost of environmental damage and other costs. Therefore, while desirable environmental goals are being postponed, it may also be appropriate to impose a tax on those fuels for which environmental restrictions are being waived. At this particular time, when energy prices are rising rapidly, we feel that it would be a mistake to add to the consumer's burden; but if progress toward independence is unsatisfactory, this option may have to be reconsidered.

See memoranda by \*OSCAR A. LUNDIN and by ROBERT B. SEMPLE, pages 83 and 84.

# 3. Supply: Independence and Redundancy

---

THERE IS NO DOUBT that in the next decade this nation will have to devote much more of its resources to increasing its energy supply than it has in the past. Investment in the major energy industries will increase rapidly, exceeding its historical share of one-fifth of gross business fixed investment. Similarly, the proportion of GNP represented by value added in the coal mining, petroleum production, and pipeline industries will grow beyond the 2½ percent recorded in 1973.

Government spending for energy will also increase. The federal government spent less than $1 billion for energy research in fiscal 1974, most of it to continue development of the fast breeder reactor. Even in fiscal 1975, twice as much federal money will be spent for space and fifty times as much for defense as will be expended for energy research and development, and only $700 million will be spent for public transportation.

### How Much Is Enough?

Which energy sources should be developed or expanded? In what sequence? How much more should be spent to develop them and by whom? The answers to these questions involve policies for energy prices and profits in the private sector and for taxes, public programs, and other government actions.

A very large U.S. investment in energy resources is justified under the present circumstances. Such investment will influence the bargaining positions of the members of OPEC. If these countries believe that reasonably priced substitutes will not be available before their oil resources are exhausted, they are likely to increase prices and curtail production. If, on the other hand, the United States makes massive investments to develop substitutes that could potentially replace imported oil at current prices, the exporting countries will find it less advantageous to hold oil in the ground.

There is much merit in the argument for redundancy in the face of uncertain energy supplies. No one knows whether large quantities of domestic oil and gas will be found in accessible places; whether moderately priced, environmentally acceptable synthetic fuels can be obtained in large quantities from the massive U.S. coal and oil shale resources; or how quickly progress will be made with breeder reactors and more exotic energy sources. New oil discoveries in the South China Sea, the North Sea, the Arctic, or elsewhere could alter the world oil market. Finally, the oil sands in Canada may greatly expand the world's energy supply.

Good fortune with only a few of these options could make the others redundant. But a prudent energy policy should seek insurance against misfortune. Thus, except for the constraint of scarce manpower or material resources, there is no need to choose between coal and nuclear power or between oil shale and coal gasification, at least until their relative costs and merits are more clearly understood.

*We believe that doing too much to achieve energy independence is a more acceptable risk than doing too little. Although priorities must be established on the basis of the time required to bring new supplies into use, many alternatives should be pursued. Implementation of this strategy may require that the government assume some of the risks, especially for higher-risk, long-term investments that are vulnerable to a sharp reduction in world oil prices.*

### Near-Term Possibilities: Familiar Fuels

The major additions to the U.S. energy supply over the next five to ten years will have to come from fuels and processes that are already in widespread use. Fortunately, the United States has substantial resources in conventional oil, natural gas, coal, and uranium, and these can be developed.

*Conventional oil* and *natural gas* are believed to exist in large quantities on the Alaskan slopes and on the outer continental shelves off both coasts and in the Gulf of Mexico. Extensive supplies of natural gas and heavy oils may also be found elsewhere in the United States. Recent estimates by the U.S. Geological Survey suggest that the nation's remaining ultimately recoverable crude oil may be as much as sixty-five times as great as current annual consumption and that similar ratios apply to natural gas.

Exploitation of these resources requires more extensive exploration to find new reserves and higher recovery rates from developed fields. Both requirements will be met if the return from producing oil and gas remains high enough to cover the additional costs of these activities and includes sufficient profit to justify the necessary investment. Rapid exploitation of oil and natural gas requires little new technology. Given profitable prices and rapid leasing of federal lands, these conventional sources could provide considerably more energy in 1985 than they do now. Substantial additional supplies may also come from intensive efforts at secondary and tertiary recovery from new and existing oil fields.

However, if a substantial increase is to be achieved before 1980, the existing bottlenecks in energy-producing equipment must be eliminated and new ones must be prevented from forming. Of immediate concern is the scarcity of pipes and drilling rigs. These shortages have generated strong pressures for the government to assume the role of arbiter or allocator not only to facilitate progress in high-priority programs but also to avoid the costly delays that characterize interruptions in production and construction schedules. Several legislative proposals to this purpose are pending in Congress.

To meet these constraints on energy-related production and construction, FEA has instituted a program of positive assistance and facilitation to industry. This program encourages voluntary cooperation by the major oil companies in sharing tubular goods with independent operators and otherwise aids in locating alternative sources of supply to meet spot shortages.

In the firm belief that market forces are the best allocator of scarce resources, we express strong support of FEA in its efforts to stimulate voluntary industry cooperation, and we urge it to step up these activities. **As a matter of foresight and prudence, we believe that the President should have clear authority to establish a system of priorities and alloca-**

tion governing critical materials and equipment required for energy production upon declaration of a national emergency caused by acute supply shortages that seriously impair U.S. energy independence objectives. This can be done by amending the National Defense Production Act of 1950 to extend current defense-related priority systems to civilian energy needs. We earnestly hope that such drastic measures will not be necessary.

## Other Available Sources of Energy

In 1972, before the embargo, domestic production of oil and natural gas accounted for 45 quads of energy, or 63 percent of U.S. consumption. Energy independence will require that other fuels provide a greater share of the nation's energy. Coal and nuclear power provide the best opportunities for reducing dependence on the fuels that are in short supply. Coal can be used directly for industrial purposes, and both fuels can replace oil and gas in the generation of electricity. In 1972, electric power represented one-third of the energy used in the nontransportation sectors of the economy; in 1950, it was one-fifth. The trend is likely to continue and even accelerate if heat pumps come into widespread use for heating and cooling.

*Coal* mined in this country could provide over 100 times as much energy as the United States consumed in 1973. Rapid exploitation of U.S. coal resources will require a large increase in both surface and underground mining. As in the case of oil and natural gas, equipment and labor bottlenecks will have to be eliminated quickly if early progress is to be made. Draglines and earth-moving equipment appear to be in especially short supply. Even the modest goal of producing 95 quads of energy by 1985 implies that 1972 coal production will have to be almost doubled. A corresponding increase in coal-haulage capacity and better ways of making surface mining environmentally acceptable are also necessary. Moreover, some efficient means must be found for removing sulfur from coal, either before, while, or after it is burned (i.e., from the flue gas). In 1972, more than 60 percent of the coal consumed in the United States was used to generate electricity, but only 42 percent of the electricity consumed was generated by coal. There is a large margin both for expanding the direct use of coal by industry and for increasing the proportion of electricity generated by coal-fired plants. However, these opportunities will be realized only if the bottleneck and environmental problems are solved.

*Nuclear power* promises to be the solution to many of the difficulties associated with fossil fuels. The absence of combustion gases means elimination of any air pollution problems, and fast breeder reactors offer the possibility of substantial relief from the danger that uranium resources will be exhausted. However, rapid growth in nuclear power will require resolution of the safety and safeguard issues to the public's satisfaction, including concerns over nuclear-waste disposal, weapons diversion, and possible accidents. It is hoped that solutions will come with more experience, thereby permitting a reduction in the present eight-to-ten-year period between project approval and plant operation. At present, nuclear power generated by light-water reactors is going through the transition from new technology to familiar energy source. Although it provides only 1 percent of the current U.S. energy supply, uranium is likely to account for a substantial portion of the nation's energy consumption by 1985. Continued growth in electricity's share of final energy demand and a shift to coal and uranium as the fuels for electric generation are essential to achieving U.S. energy independence.*

## Reducing Uncertainty

Achieving the potential afforded by domestic oil, gas, coal, and uranium resources will require a substantial reduction in the uncertainty that surrounds U.S. energy policy with regard to prices, imports, leasing of federally owned resources, and environmental standards. Uncertainty over price controls jeopardizes investment in oil exploration, and oil refineries will not be built unless supplies of crude oil are assured.

The degree of uncertainty that now characterizes the environmental situation is excessively high and should be reduced. Although citizen participation is a necessary part of environmental decisions, the multitude of jurisdictions and approvals now required makes it very difficult to plan new facilities or modify existing ones. Similarly, although there will inevitably be some modifications as scientific knowledge and political preferences change, the current state of flux in air, water, and safety standards and in the siting of facilities is inefficient. For example, it is unrealistic to expect that investments will be made to expand coal mining capacity on the basis of temporary relaxations of clean air standards.

A primary goal of government policy should be to reduce the uncertainty that now impedes fuel production. **To reduce uncertainty, we recommend leaving the price of newly discovered oil and natural gas**

See memorandum by *ELVIS J. STAHR, page 89.

uncontrolled; establishing more efficient environmental controls; stream-lining procedures for leasing federal oil, coal, shale, and natural gas resources and for siting energy facilities; and leasing environmentally acceptable sites for extraction of oil, gas, coal, and oil shale as rapidly as exploitation can be undertaken.*

Price controls on old domestic oil are another source of uncertainty and carry the potential for misallocating resources.[†] At present, about 60 percent of the domestically produced oil, or approximately 35 percent of the oil consumed in the United States, is controlled. This share will diminish as existing wells are depleted. However, valuable oil will be lost in the process because the lower price tends to discourage the application of secondary and tertiary recovery methods to some controlled wells. Furthermore, as in the case of natural gas, the lower price tends to stimulate demand for petroleum products.

In addition, the government's efforts to distribute fairly the lower-priced controlled oil create serious administrative difficulties. As a result, the oil industry is subject to a four-part control system: allocation of crude oil, allocation of petroleum products, controls on the price of old crude oil, and rules to pass through costs. Decontrol of old oil prices would put an end to the entire allocation system as well as increasing supply and decreasing demand.

In many respects, the decontrol of old oil prices is directly analogous to the decontrol of natural gas prices, which we recommended earlier. **We recommend the phased removal of price controls on old oil (for the reasons given above), but we recognize that political and social considerations may well require that "windfall profits on old oil" be taxed unless channeled into net additions to energy-producing investment dedicated to increasing supplies.**

It is obvious that domestic fuel production needs to be increased as quickly as possible if energy independence is to be achieved. This requires that industry be given the opportunity to develop the nation's energy resources without delay. Industries that supply specialized equipment for exploration need to be assured that the expanded market for their products will not disappear because of a change in leasing policy. In order to avoid the risk of oil spills, the government should ensure that only envi-

---

[†]The controlled price averages $5.25 a barrel, which is about half the uncontrolled price. The price is uncontrolled if the oil comes from stripper wells (those producing 10 barrels a day or less), from newly discovered fields, or from older property in excess of levels produced in a base period.

See memoranda by *PHILIP SPORN and by SIDNEY J. WEINBERG, JR., pages 86 and 87.

See memoranda by **THOMAS G. AYERS, by JOSEPH L. BLOCK, by JAMES R. KENNEDY, and by GEORGE C. McGHEE, pages 84 and 87.

ronmentally safe sites are developed.\* The government should also ensure that the development of onshore sites reflects rational land-use decisions, that only competent firms are permitted to operate (especially where there is environmental risk), and that leaseholders act promptly to develop resources. Performance requirements, if not already in effect, should be established so that leases revert to the government if work does not proceed at an appropriate pace. In addition, land rentals should be high enough to discourage leasing for speculative purposes. Within these objectives, leases should be granted expeditiously.

## Near-Term Trade-offs between the Environment and Increased Energy Production

There is little doubt that concern for the environment has delayed the development of oil and natural gas resources. Delay in the Alaskan pipeline reduced current oil supplies by 2 million barrels per day and delayed the search for oil and gas in that area. Offshore exploration for these fuels was slowed in the wake of the Santa Barbara spill. Environmental concerns have also prompted postponement of the construction of some nuclear facilities and some oil refineries. The gasoline consumption of some models of automobiles has increased, and the balance of energy supply and demand has been adversely affected in other ways.

The Clean Air Act made high-sulfur coal a "nonfuel," and because of more stringent health and safety standards, the price of all underground coal increased. In 1968, coal provided the energy for approximately half of the electricity generated in the United States; oil and gas provided 32 percent. By 1972, coal's share had declined by 9 percent, and most of the loss was absorbed by oil and gas. Independence requires that this trend be reversed and that coal carry a larger share of the nation's energy burden.

In *More Effective Programs for a Cleaner Environment*, we recommend that "appropriate environmental agencies carefully consider whether extremely stringent emission standards now existing or envisaged can be justified on the basis of benefit-cost comparisons." We believe that the current energy situation makes it especially important to apply this recommendation to electric power plants that utilize fossil fuels. Moreover, we suggest that, where practical, standards for the control of pollutants discharged into the air be replaced with suitably monitored ambient air standards.

See memorandum by \*GEORGE C. McGHEE, page 89.

Although concern for safety and for the environment was a factor leading to the loss of energy independence, it was not the only one. Contractor difficulties and equipment deficiencies also contributed to the delays in expanding U.S. nuclear capacity. For a variety of reasons, it has taken eight to ten years to complete an operational nuclear facility in the United States; whereas this has been accomplished in four or five years elsewhere. Similarly, increases in auto weight and accessories caused a substantial decline in gasoline efficiency. Moreover, because environmental costs had been largely ignored in the past, it was appropriate that the energy balance be worsened somewhat in order to protect the environment. Certainly, the offshore drilling practices, the Alaskan pipeline, and the automobile engines that will be in use in a few years will be less environmentally harmful than those that existed or were proposed five years ago.

A large portion of environmental restrictions deal with events that are unlikely to occur; yet, if they do occur, they will cause substantial damage. They range from possible oil spills, which primarily endanger property and wildlife, to potential nuclear accidents, which threaten human life. Every effort should be made to hold the risk to the practical minimum; there are no risk-free alternatives. Depending on imported oil or abruptly reducing the rate of energy consumption is also dangerous. The United States tolerates a transportation system that is far from perfectly safe and wiring and heating apparatus that cause accidents.

Consideration of nuclear facilities, offshore drilling, and similar energy activities should take a balanced view toward environmental risk with the objective of creating a low-risk total system. Although it is unrealistic to expect that all risk can be removed, we favor a conservative approach. It would be foolhardy to jeopardize the nuclear option or, indeed, the chances for energy independence by putting anything less than the maximum effort into nuclear safety. Consideration should be given to the safety advantages afforded by nuclear parks and to the suggestion that nuclear plants be located underground.*

## Medium-Term Possibilities:
### Synthetic Fuels and Breeder Reactors

Synthetic fuels from coal and oil shale can extend the current U.S. reliance on fossil fuels for generations. Moreover, these fuels could begin to make an important contribution to U.S. energy independence by the

See memorandum by *ELVIS J. STAHR, page 90.

second half of the 1980s if a crash program were undertaken immediately. But policy must reflect the considerable uncertainty concerning the production technology and economics and therefore the cost of these fuels.

Low-BTU gas made from coal could take the place of some portion of the natural gas now used by industry, thereby freeing that high-quality fuel for residential use. High-BTU gas could also be obtained from coal and added directly to the interstate pipelines. Technologies for both high- and low-BTU gas are available now, and construction of these plants could proceed immediately. (Plans for a number of major plants have already been announced and are awaiting FPC approval.) Although it is unlikely that more than 5 percent of the 1985 energy supply will be satisfied by synthetic fuels, an industry of that size would be able to expand rapidly in subsequent years.

It is estimated that U.S. oil shale resources could eventually produce 1 trillion barrels of oil. Large-scale production, however, will require the solution of the environmental problems created by the current production process, which substantially expands the volume of shale as it is processed. Moreover, local supplies of water may not be sufficient for large-scale processing and for reclaiming some mining areas. Development of a successful process or another technique that will moderate these problems at an acceptable cost will be necessary if the potential of these resources is to be realized. But it will take a decade or more and enormous investments before the oil shale industry is large enough to add substantially to the energy supply.

The long-term adequacy of U.S. uranium resources is not only subject to the usual uncertainties concerning the quantity of the resource and the demand for nuclear energy but also depends on nuclear technology itself. Gas-cooled reactors promise an increase in efficiency over the light-water reactors that make up most of the current generation of nuclear plants. The development of breeder reactors would mean that known uranium reserves would be sufficient well into the next century.

A great deal of uncertainty normally characterizes the energy industry; it will always have to take into account the unknown geological factors of the location of oil, gas, and uranium reserves and therefore the question of the cost and time required to develop them. This is a case in which technology is known but the location is not. The industry is now beginning to be faced with the reverse situation, in which the resource location is known but the technology is not yet available. Finding oil shale and coal resources is not difficult, but the cost and the time that will be necessary to develop the conversion industries to make oil and gas from these resources are unknown. Similar observations can be made about uranium and the breeder reactor.

One of the government's major contributions will be to reduce the uncertainties associated with the technologies for synthetic fuels and nuclear fission. **We recommend that to the extent necessary the government fund research, development, and demonstration pilot plants for synthetic fuels from oil shale and coal and also for breeder reactors and other advanced nuclear technologies. In addition, the government should support similar activities for advanced coal mining techniques and related land reclamation and for improved methods of removing sulfur from coal.**

We believe that private industry will undertake research and development of energy sources that are likely to be economic in the near term. However, the cost and availability of alternatives to oil and natural gas are likely to have strategic importance for world energy prices. Therefore, the full benefits of successful research and development in this area will far exceed the private profits accruing to the successful investor. We feel that government support for large-scale research and development is justified because of this discrepancy between private and social benefits and because the government is responsible for an adequate supply of energy overall and for the nation's progress toward independence.

The development of synthetic fuels may also require that the U.S. government offset the uncertainty over the market structures in oil caused by OPEC actions. If OPEC follows the pattern of most cartels, the market structure will change, especially if current high prices bring forth large additions to supply and reductions in demand. This possibility and the capacity of the Persian Gulf countries to make substantial profit on their oil at prices well under the cost of most substitutes make for a highly uncertain investment situation. A $700 million shale plant that can produce oil for $10.00 a barrel is a high-risk venture if a competitor can profitably sell oil for $2.00 a barrel. World oil prices may never be reduced; nevertheless, the possibility of a reduction could slow development of the expensive energy technologies that the nation needs.

The private investor may not think it prudent to depend on the permanence of the OPEC cartel, but it would be imprudent for the country to depend on its dissolution. There are a number of ways of removing the risk of lower oil prices, and they have different implications. Therefore, it is important to have criteria for selecting among them.

One criterion is maintaining incentives for efficient performance. This suggests avoiding direct government operation or cost-plus contracting of these activities. A second criterion is to avoid the situation in which the costs of these new technologies essentially set a floor for all imported and domestic energy supplies and thus weaken the incentive for lower OPEC prices. This tends to rule out the use of rigid import quotas or tariff systems that maintain a high price for all energy supplies. A third criterion is to minimize the cost of any federal subsidy which suggests that a flexible contract arrangement be made. If some technologies prove to be so effective that others are rendered superfluous, there should be some means of halting high-cost production and cutting losses by buying out the high-cost plants.

**With these criteria in mind, we recommend that the government's objective should be to ensure that industry produces substantial quantities of synthetic fuels in the shortest time feasible.** The profit potential of these new technologies may bring forth the private effort required without special government assistance. Development may proceed more rapidly if the government eliminates the risk that potential lower OPEC prices pose to private investors. **If private commitments to build adequate synthetic fuel facilities are not made very soon, the government should encourage investment by contracting to buy a substantial quantity of synthetic fuels.** Such take-or-pay contracts would set a minimum guaranteed price for the output of these synthetic fuel plants.

This would minimize the government's interference in the industry's operation. If world oil prices stayed at current levels, then the guarantee would be inoperative. If world prices fell, the government would be no more than a customer for the industry's product. For example, if the bids submitted under this procedure promised oil at a price of $10.00 per barrel and world prices were higher than that, the government need not be involved; the industry could sell its product on the open market. However, if the world price fell to $7.00, each barrel produced under this contract would require a government subsidy of $3.00. Part of the subsidy could be provided by having the government purchase synthetic fuels to meet Defense Department or other internal government needs. For the remaining output, the government might simply remit the $3.00 to the producing firms. If contracts were written to support an industry producing 3.5 quads of energy (about 1.5 million barrels per day), and if the subsidy were in fact $3.00 per barrel, the government cost would be less than $2 billion annually. On the other hand, if the presence of these industries meant that U.S. energy prices were only $.10 less per equivalent barrel than they would be otherwise, U.S. consumers would save the cost of the subsidy.

The initial decision on these contracts need be made only for the first generation of synthetic fuel plants. Subsequent decisions would be made in light of cost and operating experience with this first generation and with knowledge of price developments for competing fuels.

If contracts are let for synthetic fuels, as we recommend, and if world oil prices fall, the synthetic fuel industries will have to be subsidized. In this circumstance, the subsidy can be viewed as buying a standby source of fuel. Although it may be possible to modulate the quantity produced, these plants may have to operate near capacity in order to be viable. The output could be used to provide some of the oil stockpile and to meet the government's demand for oil. Most importantly, an operating industry of the size recommended would provide the experience and technological base that would permit rapid expansion if conditions warranted.

## Long-Term Prospects: Research

The near- and intermediate-term energy sources that we have discussed will in all likelihood provide most of the energy the United States will consume in this century. However, lead times in this field are very long. Only by starting now on the basic research programs for new energy sources can the flexibility that the nation may require in the next century be assured.

*Geothermal* and *solar* energy provide opportunities to moderate the required increase in the production of fossil fuels and nuclear energy. By 1990, the heat stored beneath the earth's crust could be providing some additional energy for electric power, and the sun's heat could be lessening the residential-commercial sector's purchases of energy. Both sources are somewhat restricted geographically: geothermal energy to those portions of the country where underground heat can be brought to the surface rather easily; solar energy to those areas where sunlight is dependable. However, solar heat can be used in much of the country to supplement conventional heating.*

The use of *solid waste* as an energy source is also promising. In addition, there are possibilities for making the generation of electricity more efficient or at least stabilizing efficiency at the current level. For the more distant future, there is the hope that fusion energy, which is independent of scarce resources, could produce a hydrogen fuel that will provide dependable, pollution-free energy.

See memorandum by *FRANKLIN A. LINDSAY, page 90.

Substantial government involvement is justified for these energy sources because they are unlikely to be very important for ten years or more and because they require considerable basic research. **The federal government should fund a substantial basic and applied research program in solar, geothermal, and fusion energy; in more efficient electric power generation; and in innovative techniques such as the use of solid waste as an energy source.\* Whenever possible, these efforts should be internationally coordinated, and the costs should be shared by participating nations.\*\*** The joint U.S.-Soviet project on magnetohydrodynamics is a step in the right direction.

There are many promising paths to be followed, given enough time and economic resources. Moreover, if a flexible policy is pursued, there is no need to choose the best alternatives at this time. A balanced research program would give the nation and the world many options.

## Capital Costs

Most energy exploitation is capital-intensive. A long and expensive period of exploration and development precedes oil production. Coal gasification and oil shale plants are so expensive to build that fixed costs per unit of output are high relative to operating costs. Shale oil plants (100,000 barrels per day) and coal gasification plants (250 million cubic feet per day) may cost $700 million or more apiece. An all-out program to build sixteen synthetic fuel plants by 1985 would cost $11 billion† and would produce less than 4 percent of the 1985 U.S. energy demand.

The bulk of the investment made over the next decade will be for increasing the supply of the familiar fuels, not for developing these new technologies. Close to $300 billion may have to be invested in order to produce enough conventional oil, natural gas, coal, and uranium to meet the 1985 demand. In addition to the capital required to develop the fuels, large sums of money are needed to generate and transmit electrical energy. The electric utility industry will require nearly $300 billion in new facilities by 1985. This sum will not be forthcoming unless the utility commissions allow rates to rise in a manner that reflects the increased costs of new plants (including the higher interest on borrowed capital) and increased fuel and operating costs.\*\*\*

---

†All investment figures are in constant 1974 dollars and apply to the period from 1971 to 1985.

See memorandum by *ELVIS J. STAHR, page 87.
See memoranda by **PHILIP SPORN and by ELVIS J. STAHR, page 88.
See memorandum by ***ROBERT D. LILLEY, page 91.

There is at least one area in which the government can properly act to reduce financial requirements and at the same time eliminate some unnecessary uncertainty. In fiscal 1975, the energy industry is expected to pay $8 billion to the government for leases to the outer continental shelves that contain potential oil and gas reserves, an amount greater than that spent for exploration within the United States. Substantial funds will also be spent for onshore oil and shale leases. This large amount of front-end money increases the industry's financial needs and inhibits risk taking (thus, the frequent appearance of multifirm consortia in the bidding). **We recommend that the front-end costs of oil and gas leases be reduced in return for an appropriately designed formula for higher payments on the oil and gas extracted from successfully developed leases.**[*] A simple royalty payment tends to shorten the economic life of an oil well and, therefore, would *not* be an appropriate formula. However, a declining royalty or one based on marginal extraction cost would reduce the front-end cost without this drawback.

A total of $600 to $700 billion is a modest estimate for the investment required over the period from 1971 to 1985 for the energy facilities we have described; it amounts to approximately one-quarter of the country's projected business fixed investment for this period. The creation of these energy-producing facilities, by itself, will require at least 0.5 percent more of GNP than the United States has been spending for these purposes.

In addition to the substantial investment required to increase the supply of energy, major financial resources will be required to moderate the demand for energy. New production capacity will be required to produce more efficient autos, homes, industrial equipment, and so on. These requirements, added to the capital required to meet environmental goals and to expand the country's productive capacity, will pose severe problems for economic policy.

It is impossible to foretell which capital investments will most reduce U.S. dependence on imports. In many cases, the investment required to eliminate 1 quad of energy demand through conservation will be less than that required to add an equal amount to supply. In the absence of other distortions, free capital markets will generally direct capital flows to their most profitable uses. However, the problem of raising funds for the investments we have suggested will have to be solved in the historically unique situation that will evolve as the oil-exporting nations accumulate vast financial surpluses. Much of the OPEC surplus, estimated to be running at $65 billion in 1974, or 4.6 percent of U.S. GNP, is being invested

See memorandum by *IAN MacGREGOR, page 87.

in short-term assets. These circumstances will tax the capacity of financial markets to mediate between short-term lenders and long-term borrowers and across national boundaries. Because of the importance of these problems, this Committee is undertaking the task of producing a policy statement that will contain specific recommendations for meeting the country's overall capital needs.

## Reserves and Standby Capacity

Because it would be foolhardy not to prepare for a repetition of the 1973–1974 embargo, we recommend in Chapter 2 that standby energy sources be developed as protection against possible emergencies. It makes economic sense for private industry to hold expensive inventories and maintain backup equipment in order to avoid the risk of having to curtail production because an essential input might become unavailable. Similarly, it makes economic sense for the nation to incur the expense of standby energy sources, especially because their presence may moderate OPEC price demands.

To be useful, the standby arrangement must be able to provide energy immediately upon the initiation of an embargo and for as long as may be necessary. These arrangements will have to include an efficient combination of stockpiles of crude oil and refined petroleum products, plans to switch from oil to coal, and plans to increase production on an emergency basis from either working or shut-in oil fields. A state of readiness at these facilities should follow a continuously updated plan to provide an orderly transition to standby sources in an emergency. This plan must include adequate domestic refinery and distribution capability in the event that imports of petroleum products are interrupted. The extent of standby sources should depend on the risk that a second embargo will occur, the cost to the U.S. economy of reduced petroleum availability, and the minimum cost of creating and maintaining standby capacity.*

If world prices fall, it will become economic to tolerate more imports and provide more standby facilities; but this circumstance, if and when it occurs, should not be permitted to lead to a reduction in U.S. efforts to expand domestic producing capacity. At this time, when imports account for nearly 40 percent of consumption and world prices are more than $10 a barrel, there is little danger that standby capacity will discourage domestic efforts.

See memorandum by *GEORGE C. McGHEE, page 71.

# 4. Government Organization for Energy Administration

THE FEDERAL GOVERNMENT'S HANDLING of energy matters has long suffered from diffusion, narrow perspectives, and lack of adequate data. Jurisdiction has been divided among a bewildering maze of agencies operating without a unifying energy strategy or an integrated administrative structure. A recent Senate study identified forty-six federal agencies with direct responsibility for some portion of the energy system and eighteen others whose policies substantially influence it. Moreover, in the zoning and siting of energy facilities, the policies of federal agencies are frequently at cross-purposes with state and local policies. These difficulties have been further compounded by a fragmented committee organization for energy-related legislation in Congress.

Because of the dispersion of responsibility and lack of an effective early-warning system, government policy makers were unprepared to cope with the sudden oil embargo in the fall of 1973. As a result of the emergency, the government took a number of actions to bring some semblance of coordination and direction to federal energy activities. Project Independence was promulgated in November 1973, and many legislative proposals were drafted to alleviate the energy shortage and to bring about the effective administration of energy policy. Emergency powers were given to the hastily organized Federal Energy Office, which has now been superseded by FEA. A cabinet-level committee on energy was established by the President in June 1974.

These steps were not an adequate response to the crisis situation. There was no coherent strategy, and coordinating mechanisms remained weak. These shortcomings are still present. FEA has been making some progress in maintaining a continuous assessment of the energy problem and in taking necessary crisis actions. But it lacks the status of a major cabinet department and does not possess the principal instruments of federal energy control and operations. Perhaps most serious has been the diverse and sometimes contradictory views expressed by the secretaries of the Departments of the Treasury, Interior, and State, the FEA administrator, and other top government officials on energy matters, particularly regarding oil imports, pricing, and taxes.

Recently, however, the government has taken a number of constructive steps. The Energy Reorganization Act of 1974 brought into being ERC, ERDA, and NRC, consolidating many vital functions. The President has also mandated a revitalized conservation program. Nevertheless, although we are encouraged by these recent developments, we believe that still further steps are urgently required. In our view, *a thoroughly revamped and strengthened organization and system for setting and implementing federal energy policy is a prerequisite for achieving energy independence.* To this end, we support proposals for the creation of a department of energy and natural resources.

## The President and Energy Policy

For the next several years, energy policy must rank high on the President's agenda. Indeed, there will be few actions in the field of domestic or international affairs requiring a presidential decision that will not involve energy considerations. The absence of an effective coordinating mechanism for synthesizing energy policy at the level of presidential decision making has been one of the major inadequacies of executive leadership since the beginning of the energy shortage.

For this reason, we commend both the recent action of Congress establishing ERC and the prompt action of the President in designating the secretary of the interior as its chairman. (The Energy Reorganization Act of 1974 wisely provides that the council shall be terminated upon enactment of a permanent department responsible for energy and natural resources or two years after the council's creation, whichever is the shorter term.) These are important steps toward effectively organizing the structure of government for energy policy and action and shaping its program for reducing oil imports and expanding energy supplies. In appointing the secretary of the interior chairman of the new council, the President apparently intends to vest policy leadership for the executive branch in this cabinet officer. This in no way relieves the President of basic decision-making responsibilities, nor should it preempt other cabinet officers from advocacy within their respective jurisdictions. But it can be expected that major policy issues will now be resolved within the structure of the council and that henceforth the government will speak with a clear, confident, and unified voice on energy matters.

We support the President's mandate to ERC for the reduction of oil imports by 1 million barrels a day by the end of 1975. We believe this is a modest goal that can be achieved with no more than marginal disruption to the nation's living standards. The government should be prepared to call for even more severe restrictions on energy use if circumstances require.

Under the guidance and impetus of the council, the government's present inchoate conservation program must be recast and revitalized. We believe that FEA is the agency best suited at this time to fulfilling this role. With FEA providing leadership, other agencies of the government can also play an important role in developing and administering energy-conservation programs affecting their particular sectors of the economy. The General Services Administration is already well advanced in promoting and implementing a program designed to reduce energy consumption in and by all federal agencies. FEA should monitor the entire federal effort, arranging for necessary research where appropriate and fostering a forceful program to economize the use of energy. An office of energy conservation should be established in each of the Departments of Transportation, Commerce, and Housing and Urban Development. Under the guidance of FEA, these should have responsibility for programs directed to improving efficiency in the transportation, industrial, and residential and commercial sectors.

## Accelerating Research and Development

The enactment of legislation in October 1974 creating ERDA represents a major step in the direction of energy independence. Historically, energy research and development (except for nuclear development) has been uncoordinated, fragmented, uneven, and underfinanced. Its scale and organization were inadequate to cope with the demands imposed by the present energy situation and its future requirements.

ERDA will now appropriately consolidate existing research and development programs into a single executive agency and multiply the availability of appropriated funds. The programs include the research activities of the Department of the Interior and the Atomic Energy Commission and also some of those that have been the responsibility of EPA and the National Science Foundation. In developing a consolidated program, the new agency should seek to create healthy competition among various alternative sources of energy. ERDA should end the favored status of nuclear technology at the same time that it utilizes the administrative and technical expertise of AEC in managing large-scale research.*

The capacity for independence from uncertain imports will depend importantly on successfully translating developed technology into production capacity. Entirely new industries must be created to produce and market new sources of power. Government involvement will probably be needed to guarantee the commercial availability of such new energy sources.

To obtain full-scale production promptly once advanced technology has been developed, it may be necessary to establish a new organization that will have the authority for transforming ERDA's successful prototype developments into viable commercial endeavors. This effort might embody roles and functions paralleling the Reconstruction Finance Corporation of the 1930s. In earlier chapters, we suggest that the government may have a role to play in supporting production of synthetic fuels by private industry, especially if there is a possibility that world oil prices might fall. Contracting for and disposing of these fuels could become an essential government responsibility.

ERDA legislation properly stipulates the governing authority and policies of the administrator in discharging his responsibilities for expanding energy production while giving suitable consideration to the economic, social, and environmental consequences of new technology. In our view, the Energy Reorganization Act itself adequately establishes policy guidelines to assure proper protection of social and environmental objectives while pursuing essential research and development measures for energy independence. Within these broad policies, the President and administrator should be given wide latitude to adapt program priorities and operating policies suitable to developing and swiftly changing national requirements, unhampered by rigid legislated guidelines.

See memorandum by *THOMAS G. AYERS, page 91.

### Energy Regulation

Another constructive action that the government has taken in recent months is the creation of NRC incident to the creation of ERDA and the dissolution of AEC. It is widely recognized that AEC's regulatory and promotional functions were incongruous and led to conflicts of interest because they were combined in the same agency. We welcome the creation of NRC and hope that it will evolve into a positive force for energy development while scrupulously preserving essential safety standards.

Although we are encouraged by this action, we believe that the government's overall regulatory system is in grave need of a major overhaul. Current regulatory processes lack coordination with national economic policy and are burdened with adjudicative procedures more suited to the nineteenth century than to contemporary times. There are wide divergences in the formulation and application of policy. Regulatory decisions reflect a single energy source rather than a broad perspective and seldom respond to crises with the requisite urgency, flexibility, or incisiveness. These deficiencies are compounded by the myriad state and local agencies exercising regulatory powers. The resulting problems for the industry are at least partially responsible for the time required to bring nuclear plants into operation and for the uncertainty that has discouraged investment in energy facilities.

Accordingly, we welcome the President's initiative in outlining to Congress, on October 8, 1974, his proposal for the establishment of a national commission on regulatory reform. With respect to energy affairs, we urge that such a commission direct its efforts to simplifying requirements, terminating obsolete or uneconomic restraints, and establishing where possible a one- or two-step approval mechanism for all energy facilities. The process involved in licensing and in approving sites is now protracted and redundant; it is vitally important that this be expedited. We have no illusions about the difficulty of achieving this reform, but we believe that remedy is of critical importance at the federal level as well as in state and local jurisdictions.

In the Energy Reorganization Act, Congress invites the President to submit further recommendations concerning energy organization, including the option of "consolidation in whole or part of regulatory functions concerning energy." We are convinced that national regulatory policies would benefit from the perspective provided by a comprehensive agency embracing all energy forms in a single, unified structure. Unification could also advance the goals of simplifying procedures and developing a rational and consistent (but not necessarily uniform) regulatory pattern for energy sources and uses.

## Department of Energy and Natural Resources

It is evident that the government is gearing up to meet the energy challenge. Nevertheless, further essential organizational reform is required if the nation is to make speedy progress toward energy independence. In this Committee's view, the most urgent requirement is to establish a cabinet-level organization that provides comprehensive overview and administration of the government's energy functions. **We urge that the President and Congress move as rapidly as possible to create a department of energy and natural resources in order to achieve an integrated structure for energy administration in the federal government, which is essential to achieving energy independence.**\*

In a message to Congress in March 1971, President Nixon proposed such a unified, consolidated department with responsibility for administering energy and mineral resources; land and recreation resources; water resources; oceanic, atmospheric, and earth sciences; and Indian and territorial affairs. In the absence of forceful support from the administration, congressional hearings were inconclusive and no action was taken on the proposed department.

The original proposal must now be updated and adapted, but the concept of forming such a department offers a sound framework for properly integrating and coordinating related land, water, energy, and environmental protection programs. Many conflicting interests clearly are involved, and profound political opposition to this proposal can be anticipated. Nevertheless, because the stakes are so high, we concur in the view that this vital reform must no longer be considered a long-range proposal; it must be adopted at the earliest date possible. (The Energy Reorganization Act of 1974 calls on the President to formulate an explicit plan for the organization of energy and related functions as soon as possible but not later than June 30, 1975.)

The Department of the Interior will form the nucleus of this new department, and a substantial part of its operations will consist of long-established Interior Department bureaus. We believe that it will be a mistake if the new department is simply formed and operated as a retread of the old department for the following reasons: Interior has long been oriented to development of hydroelectric power and to the fossil fuels

See memoranda by \*JOHN B. CAVE, by FRANKLIN A. LINDSAY, and by PHILIP SPORN, pages 78 and 79.

industry; the new department must now greatly expand its horizons to include other forms of energy production. Interior traditionally has been preoccupied with resource supply; the energy and natural resources department must now equip itself to deal aggressively with resource conservation and use. Interior has been concerned largely with short-term operations; the new department must now become more concerned with planning and with broad strategies affecting the long-term future. Interior has been traditionally devoted to the development and exploitation of natural resources; the new department must now become more firmly committed to the contemporary environmental ethic. Finally, Interior has not been notable for vigorous and progressive management; it must now mobilize itself to operate according to the highest standards of effective administration.

Although it is appropriate that the proposed department incorporate ERDA as one of its major components, it would be wise to maintain ERDA as an independent agency until the new department is well established and reoriented. This will give ERDA an opportunity to acquire status and to develop its important role. It will also provide time for intelligent resolution of the issue of ultimate responsibility for military-related nuclear research. We believe this activity should be transferred to the Department of Defense, but separating military functions from those that have civilian applications requires careful study which should be completed before further organizational adjustments are made.

### Energy and Mineral Resources Administration

The reorganization plan of 1971 included the creation of an energy and mineral resources administration as a major component of the new department of energy and natural resources. A number of agencies from the Department of the Interior, including the Bureau of Mines and the Office of Oil and Gas, were to be incorporated in this new administration.[†] Clearly, the composition and functions of an energy and mineral resources administration must be updated in order to conform with the present situation. But we believe it essential that the secretary of the department of

---

[†]The reorganization plan would locate the nonfuel-mineral activities of the transferred agencies with their energy-mineral counterparts. Separation would unnecessarily disrupt existing organizations and would bring no particular benefits to either energy or minerals.

energy and natural resources and his energy administrator have direct control of the principal elements necessary for planning, directing, and operating the government's energy production and conservation program.

It is also essential that FEA be transferred to the proposed administration as its central planning, coordinating, and directing unit. FEA's authority expires in May 1976, but its emergency powers and functions should be continued and vested in the energy and mineral resources administration. Likewise, we suggest that consideration be given to transferring the government's direct energy operations to the new administration, as recommended in 1971 by the President's Advisory Council on Executive Organization.

Although we believe that the secretary of the department of energy and natural resources should be designated the senior energy administrator of the government, the energy and mineral resources administration, as the primary supportive agency, will also require leadership of the highest quality with undersecretary status.

## Integration of Environmental Protection and Resource Development at the Cabinet Level

Current national values properly assign a high priority to the protection of the environment and to the abatement of land, air, and water pollution. The new environmental ethic has come to be accepted as a salient factor in determining the pattern of social and economic progress.

Resource administration inescapably involves the resolution of conflicts between different philosophies and objectives. Just as potential environmental damage must be assessed when resource development programs are formulated, so must the consequences of a stringent pollution abatement policy be evaluated in terms of limited energy supplies and escalating costs. The diverse interacting components of the total resource function must be reconciled at both policy and operating levels through accommodations that assure a balanced use of land, air, and water.

Under present structural arrangements, environmental and developmental objectives can be reconciled only at the presidential level. Because both CEQ and EPA are independent entities, there is no sustaining policy bridge between the environmental agencies and the resource administration agencies, principally the Department of the Interior. Furthermore, there is a natural limit on appeals for presidential decisions, and thus there is often indecision or a stalemate when urgent action is required.

This adversary relationship among agencies and a department is extremely ill suited to crisis administration.

**To balance resource use with environmental-quality objectives, we recommend that EPA be transferred to the department of energy and natural resources as a distinct and major entity of the proposed department. We believe that EPA should be coordinate with, not subordinate to, the energy and mineral resources administration and should be given status and influence commensurate with its important mission.\* We also recommend that the Council on Environmental Quality be retained in the Executive Office of the President as an independent monitor of environmental impact, serving as an advisor to the President, but without regulatory or operational responsibilities.\*\***

Such an arrangement would permit the secretary of the department of energy and natural resources, as chief of a multifunctional organization serving a broad constituency and equally and positively concerned with resource exploitation, conservation, and environmental quality to reconcile environmental protection standards with energy imperatives. An example of the need for such reconciliation is establishment of permissible emission levels for widespread reconversion of power plants to the use of coal.

This arrangement would also shelter the President from continuous pressure to accommodate policies and resolve conflicts on particular programs or projects. The federal organization should be structured to assure that only policy issues of transcendent importance can demand presidential intervention.

## Congressional Organization for Legislative Policy on Energy

There is insistent need for modernizing congressional structures and processes for energy legislation and oversight. As the committee system now operates, deliberations on energy matters are segmented, confusing, and often conflicting. In the House, primary responsibility for energy legislation resides in no less than seven committees as well as the Joint Committee on Atomic Energy; secondary responsibilities are exercised by six other House committees.† In addition, the House Appropriations Commit-

---

†House committees with primary energy jurisdiction include Government Operations, Interior and Insular Affairs, Interstate and Foreign Commerce, Merchant Marine and Fisheries, Public Works, and Ways and Means; those with secondary jurisdiction in-

See memorandum by \*JOHN R. COLEMAN, page 79.
See memorandum by \*\*ELVIS J. STAHR, page 79.

tee, through five of its subcommittees, exercises a large degree of control over the implementation of energy decisions. A similar situation exists in the Senate.[†] Thus, problems demanding a broad policy approach are handled piecemeal by the many autonomous committees and their innumerable subcommittees.

In the policy statement *Making Congress More Effective* (1970), we called attention to the fragmented congressional committee structure. The House Select Committee on Committees (chaired by Congressman Bolling), in its 1974 report, recommended consolidating legislative jurisdicition for energy policy in a major House committee on energy and environment.[††] **We endorse the much-needed consolidation of House committees on energy policy, which would unify the natural resource function. We also recommend a parallel Senate committee on energy, natural resources, and environment.** Such action would bring congressional organization more in line with the unified structure recommended for the executive branch.

**In order to further rationalize congressional jurisdiction over energy legislation, we recommend creation of a joint energy and environment committee.** Such a joint committee, equipped with reliable economic information and the ability to evaluate the effectiveness of energy administration and regulation, would be able to formulate energy policy more adequately than is now the case.

The proposed joint committee on energy and environment would assume jurisdiction over all mineral resources and their leasing, manage-

---

clude Armed Services, Banking and Currency, Education and Labor, Foreign Affairs, Judiciary, and Science and Astronautics. See U.S. Congress. House, *Committee Reform Amendments of 1974; Report of the Select Committee on Committees of the House* (Washington, D.C.: U.S. Government Printing Office, 1974), pp. 247–255.

[†]Senate committees with major energy jurisdiction include Commerce, Finance, Foreign Relations, Interior and Insular Affairs, Labor and Public Welfare, and Public Works; committees with secondary jurisdiction include Aeronautical and Space Sciences, Armed Services, Banking, and Housing and Urban Affairs. See U.S. Congress. Senate, *Major Energy Related Legislation Pending or Acted on by the 93rd Congress* (Washington, D.C.: U.S. Government Printing Office, 1974), pp. 3–71.

[††]The Bolling committee proposals were superseded by a compromise and less comprehensive proposal authored by a Democratic caucus committee headed by Congresswoman Julia Butler Hansen and approved by the House of Representatives on October 8, 1974. The only change affecting energy and environment was the transfer of research and development legislation (except nuclear) from the Committees on Interstate and Foreign Commerce, Interior and Insular Affairs, Merchant Marine and Fisheries, and Public Works to the Committee on Science and Astronautics.

ment, and transportation on public land; regulation of the energy industry; supervision of nonmilitary nuclear programs; and, of course, energy research and development. In addition, the joint committee would exercise oversight of the underdeveloped naval petroleum reserves and oil shale reserves.[†]

---

[†]Related antitrust policy would remain in the House and Senate Judiciary committees; tax policy, in the House Ways and Means Committee; and foreign economic and foreign policy, in the House Foreign Affairs Committee and the Senate Foreign Relations Committee.

# Memoranda of Comment, Reservation, or Dissent

70

*Page 13, by* JAMES Q. RIORDAN, *with which* C. WREDE PETERSMEYER
*has asked to be associated*

I support the publication of this policy statement because on balance it makes a positive contribution to the development of a national energy policy. The statement emphasizes the urgent need for additional indigenous production (as well as improved efficiency in energy use and conservation). It reaffirms the need to consider the costs of alternative environmental proposals so that we can avoid rushing into uneconomic programs that do more harm than good for the nation.

The statement urges the government to get on with the job of setting a national energy policy because we face a real and urgent problem, not a rigged or phony problem. It argues for a redundancy of efforts to increase domestic energy supply sources so that we can be sure that such supplies will begin to grow faster than domestic consumption. It makes clear the cruel hoax that is implied in no-growth solutions.

I approve the statement "on balance" because I am less than fully satisfied with it in a number of particulars. Throughout the statement, there are a number of fuzzy references to "blackmail," "windfall," "equity," and similar words. Typically, the paragraphs containing these words are more visceral than analytical. A number of these paragraphs also imply that since the current energy regime (which happily still relies in large part on private effort) is not working perfectly, a "new partnership" with government is required. That "new partnership" is evidently to mean more pervasive involvement by government through new regulations, sophisticated tax changes, and involved subsidies. The fact is, however, that there is already too much counterproductive involvement and control by government in the energy field. The statement makes a compelling case for deregulation of natural gas and oil, less restrictive laws relating to the development and use of coal, faster action by government in approving nuclear power projects, and more realistic and prompter approval of utility rate increases. Each specific case cited makes clear the need for government to stick to general policy and to avoid controls and detailed tinkering in the hope of fine tuning the free play of the market. The government-control road (as in the case of natural gas) has always been paved with good intentions, but it leads to shortage, not equity. Experience has shown us that greater reliance on a free market, even an imperfect free market, will achieve equity a good deal better than will increased regulation, complicated law, and increased bureaucracy. In the process, the free market is also likely to produce the additional domestic energy that we need.

*Page 14, by* ROBERT B. SEMPLE

Later in this statement, on page 28, we indicate that we should establish more efficient environmental controls as a means of increasing production; and on page 41, we state that "some worthwhile environmental goals may have to be postponed until a better energy balance is achieved. Some loosening of environmental standards will be necessary if the nation's coal resources are to be fully utilized." To my mind, these are important aspects of the solution to the energy crisis and our economic problems in the near term. They should have been included in this summary and emphasized in the section outlining the Committee's major recommendations. I would add that in view of the many problems facing our economy, some environmental goals will *have* to be postponed if we are to avoid even more serious problems, and this was true even before the energy crisis was thrust upon us.

*Page 14, by* FRAZAR B. WILDE

We recommend the need of leadership to convince the public of the benefits of energy independence. This is a nice phrase but is not sufficient for the total needs of the present situation.

The public is not yet convinced that we are in danger of a real energy shortage. Accordingly, they are by all accounts returning to their original speed-driving habits and reading with pleasure that currently gasoline is in good supply.

The danger to this country and to the world of the huge development of trade deficits and the unbelievable reserves being accumulated by the OPEC nations is not a subject of either knowledge or interest to the man in the street. The only way we will save our situation in the longer run is by specific controls (either refundable gas taxes or coupons) and maximum action on Project Independence, and we ought to say so without equivocation.

Our fundamental recommendations should not be weakened by our warning about jeopardizing the international economy or endangering the environment. It does not belong in this policy statement.

*Pages 14, 25, and 56, by* GEORGE C. McGHEE

Although stocks of crude oil and refined products must be maintained at a suitable determined minimum level, further drastic increases in conventional storage to take care of another possible Arab oil embargo are both costly and require scarce steel. It could never, in any event, provide insurance against a long embargo. Saudi Arabia, with its present monetary reserves, could live with an embargo indefinitely — for years. To meet such an embargo, conventional storage must be augmented by excess productive capacity that is not now available. This could be obtained by preparing for production (but not producing) existing or indicated naval reserves, particularly that in the North Slope, or other indicated reserves under federal leases. This could be done under contract with private companies with wells drilled at close spacing into producing zones that have both high productive capacity and backup reserves which could last through any expected embargo.

### Page 15, by PHILIP SPORN

The entire opening statement troubles me because it is too diffuse and does not convey the sense of grave urgency with which we are confronted. There follows my rewrite of it to fulfill this requirement more closely.

The United States is in an unprecedented energy crisis that it refuses to recognize and to take measures against consistent with its gravity and its threat to our national safety, economy, and way of life.

We are perhaps confronted by the need completely to redirect our national course on a new theory of economics and society that would not be consumption- (market-) oriented, but rather resource- and environment-oriented. We may, in fact, be entering an energy age of limited availability and delimited applicability — a sharp change for our society, which has developed under a consumption orientation and which has brought us to the preeminent position we hold today, although somewhat precariously, in production, social, and economic welfare.

Recognizing the stark reality of the current crisis and the threat of its continuance to our national life, we must accept and adopt as the means of saving ourselves the earliest possible completion of Project Independence. To implement that and to counter the threat to our society and to the entire Western world implicit in a disruption in our energy supply and its burgeoning economic burden, we must: (a) reduce our rate of growth of energy use and firmly, but without threat or bluster, put a limit on the short-term and long-term use of energy, particularly of oil; (b) expand our indigenous sources of oil and gas from our present supplies by intensified stripper operations on old wells and drilling of new offshore wells and by conversion, as technology and economics make feasible, of coal, tar sands, and oil shales to liquids, high-BTU gas, and low-BTU gas; (c) carry out a major expansion of our mining and our direct burn of solid fossil fuels — coal, that is, in its various forms — and nuclear fuel, the only two indigenous fuels we can rely on for assured availability; (d) carry through a major selective program of research and development oriented to speed the achievement of Project Independence while never losing sight of the Damoclean threat overhanging this nation as long as the energy crisis continues.

This statement is designed to develop the details of the program here outlined in as succinct a form as possible.

*Page 15, by* PHILIP SPORN

I believe this is a superficial observation. The actions of OPEC are far from unpredictable. On the contrary, having established its ability to disrupt our society by shutting off the oil spigot, OPEC will inevitably and recurrently be tempted to do so again on lesser or even no provocation.

*Page 15, by* E. SHERMAN ADAMS, *with which* LINCOLN GORDON, GILBERT E. JONES, ROBERT R. NATHAN, *and* ELVIS J. STAHR *have asked to be associated*

Energy conservation is not simply "the quickest and surest path" to reduced dependence on Arab oil; it is the *only* effective short-term means available for dealing with the energy crisis. The unavoidable implications of this fact are as follows:

Voluntary conservation measures are all to the good, of course, but they clearly cannot be counted on to do the job that needs to be done. We urgently need not only to reduce our consumption of imported oil but we must build up an emergency reserve at the same time. No one has yet suggested how these goals can be accomplished without increasing the price of gasoline used for nonessential purposes, particularly nonessential driving.

This does not imply a flat, across-the-board tax on gasoline which would be inflationary and inequitable. There are various alternative ways to provide a reasonable degree of equity while reinforcing the incentives for conservation. For example, persons who must commute to work by car could be exempted from the tax on the quantity of gas needed for that purpose.

Such a tax appears to be the only way to reduce oil consumption rapidly, to build reserves for an emergency, and to demonstrate to the oil cartel our determination to achieve energy independence. In addition, revenues from the tax could be used to subsidize public transportation, thereby reducing living costs for many people and further conserving energy.

*Page 18, by* THOMAS G. AYERS

I regard this sentence as inconsistent with the italicized statement in the following paragraph.

*Page 18, by* SHEARON HARRIS, *with which* ROBERT B. SEMPLE *has asked to be associated*

The policy statement would make a more effective contribution if it identified more clearly and specifically the serious barriers to achievement of electricity's role: that is, limited access to capital and environmental restraints.

*Page 19, by* ELVIS J. STAHR

I believe that a crash program in solar energy, such as has just been suggested for the next generation of nuclear reactors, can achieve comparable success in a comparable time frame; thus, widespread use of solar energy (and, for that matter, wind and geothermal energy) *need not* be much, if any, "farther off." My reasons for urging such a crash program are summarized briefly in a later comment relating to page 49.

*Page 19, by* IAN MacGREGOR, *with which* LINCOLN GORDON, JOHN D. HARPER, GILBERT E. JONES, *and* C. WREDE PETERSMEYER *have asked to be associated*

On the whole, this policy statement is an excellent one. It puts the emphasis where it should be: on the policies that now need to be adopted and followed by the United States. CED has admirably resisted the temptation that is so faddish today to drift into computer printouts of alternative scenarios that might be followed and that, even at the highest levels of government, have accounted for nearly a year's delay in coming to policy determinations and in other respects are obscuring the public understanding of the essentials of the energy problem.

In my view, however, the statement is unfortunately deficient in one important respect: It fails to stress the importance of the rapid expansion of production of domestic coal, especially Western coal, which could contribute so greatly to achieving the energy independence that CED seeks.

For example, under the heading of "Near-Term Possibilities" (pages 43–45), only "conventional oil and natural gas" are considered as "familiar fuels." Coal is relegated to a paragraph on page 45 under the heading "Other Available Sources of Energy." Unfortunately, the report has missed the opportunity to direct public policy attention to the most familiar fuel, coal, the supply of which can be expanded relatively quickly provided that highest priorities are assigned to this objective. Discussion of the potential for expanding U.S. coal production in that paragraph is entirely inadequate. Although there is a reference to the implication that 1972 coal production might be almost doubled if certain CED goals were to be reached, CED has failed to seize the opportunity to *recommend* that the doubling of U.S. coal production is the most immediately available near-term contributor to the reduction of our energy problem. Finally, this paragraph ends with a reference to the equipment bottlenecks and environmental problems still to be solved if coal production is to be expanded, without making any recommendations as to how they should be solved.

I believe that surface mining of coal can be carried out with entirely acceptable reclamation, especially by large-scale, well-capitalized companies. The Western coals are available in substantial quantities; they have very low sulfur content; they can be mined with a minimum of manpower problems. The Western deposits are so thick that they can be mined without disturbing more than relatively small acreages for a temporary period of from three to five years before reclamation.

Relative to capital costs alone, the expansion of domestic coal production and all the associated transport, reclamation, and community infrastructure requirements can be achieved at a fraction of the capital cost of synthetic oil or gas from coal or oil from shale. Perhaps as little as one-fourth to one-fifth as much capital cost is required for equivalent BTU output of coal for burning.

## Page 22, by PHILIP SPORN

As to the first dimension, I would think that the threat of destabilizing our economic system with its sequential adverse effect on our military security would be a far greater one than the threat either to our foreign policy or directly to our military security.

*Page 23, by* FRAZAR B. WILDE

Project Independence, if pushed vigorously, will largely reduce the risk of political blackmail or the balance-of-payments problem for the United States.

*Page 23, by* FRAZAR B. WILDE

This paragraph at best is highly debatable. Our balance-of-payments structure can and should be made favorable by two things: (1) a sharp reduction in importation of oil through specific conservation measures and (2) an early reduction in the rate of inflation in this country, which the administration claims is its number-one priority. If we reduce inflation and prices, as we must, and increase our exports, including agricultural products, we will have a modest trade deficit (if any) unless we increase foreign military activities and aid.

The investment choices of the OPEC nations and the arrangements made to recycle their funds are too uncertain and complicated to discuss here other than to express a hope for a constructive world plan through the World Bank and International Monetary Fund. The best solution for recycling is spelled out in this statement: Reduce the oil deficit and world prices.

*Page 23, by* PHILIP SPORN

As regards the alternative energy sources mentioned, the times within which they can become significantly effective are so different for conservation measures, nuclear energy, and solar energy that to bracket them is on a par with adding horses, apples, and bathtubs.

*Page 23, by* ELVIS J. STAHR

One of my principal reasons for urging a crash program in solar, wind, and geothermal energy rather than nuclear energy is that I do not believe nuclear energy *can*, as a practical matter, "be used throughout the world." Few, indeed, of the developing countries, in which most of the earth's inhabitants will be living, have either the scientific capability or the political organization or stability to cope with the enormous safety problems involved in nuclear energy systems, including the transport, processing, and storage of nuclear material. The United States still has serious unsolved problems in these respects, in spite of the availability here of many of the world's most competent scientists and engineers and a well-disciplined, well-financed nuclear energy system. Very few of the developing countries have coal, petroleum, or uranium. Virtually all of them have abundant sunshine, as do we, and solar technology is safe and thus exportable. The fuel source itself is both inexhaustible and free.

### Page 24, by PHILIP SPORN

As regards the preservation of the market-price system: This is an interesting objective, but the market-price system in energy disappeared with the October 1973 embargo. It is nonexistent today.

### Page 25, by JOHN D. GRAY (Omark Industries)

In private or government funding of new energy-producing sources or funding of new energy source research projects, it is urged that all parties involved develop an understanding of "net energy" produced or hoped to be produced and that most funding be directed into those production and/or research projects which promise the highest "net energy" output.

### Pages 25 and 32, by PHILIP SPORN

I am heartily in accord with the recommendation that the government should provide a petroleum storage system for emergencies, and I would like to put some flesh on the bones of that recommendation.

If we assume the possible energy supply and demand patterns for 1985 postulated in the table on page 16, and if we further assume that we provide storage to take care of 120 days of oil imports, or roughly $3 \times 10^{15}$ BTU (but it might on subsequent experience prove desirable to double, and possibly later, even redouble this quantity), this would mean storage of 500 million barrels of oil. Although this storage might be put together at a single location, there is good argument for dividing it on an arrangement that balances geographic location against the differences in cost of the storage facility between various locations.

Probably the most economic storage areas are those that can provide underground facilities in mined-out or excavated salt beds, and for this purpose, a number of areas on the Gulf Coast are available. Underground storage in such a location can probably be provided at a cost not to exceed $1 per barrel. The Gulf Coast also has the advantage of being a center for a radiating network of pipelines, making possible the economic transmission of the oil to most of the rest of the country.

If, now, you assume that 400 million barrels of the total of 500 million would be put in the Gulf storage area, a logical locus for the 100 million block of oil would be the West Coast, where Alaskan oil could be brought in very reasonably. Since there are no salt deposit areas on the West Coast, the chances are this would have to be a steel tank farm, and here the storage costs would run to $4 per barrel or possibly slightly higher. Thus, the total storage facilities would amount to $800 million. With oil at $10 a barrel, the oil would represent a frozen investment of $5 billion; and in rounded figures, the total project cost would be $6 billion, which is not too high a price to pay for what would be obtained in protection to the economy in case of a short-term emergency.

*Pages 26 and 62, by* JOHN B. CAVE, *with which* GILBERT E. JONES *has asked to be associated*

I am concerned with the recommendation that a new cabinet-level department be formed to handle all energy matters. Although I in no way consider myself expert in the affairs of the federal government, it seems wasteful from both manpower and time standpoints to attempt to form another cabinet-level department. History shows that it takes many months, and sometimes years, to steer a new department through Congress; and even after it is formed, there is usually some substantial time lapse before it becomes effective. In my judgment, the energy matter is sufficiently important that it should be assigned to a present cabinet-level department (Interior or Commerce) which could be strengthened and revitalized to assume the additional duties.

*Pages 26 and 62, by* PHILIP SPORN

The linking up of energy and natural resources into a single department, presumably headed by a cabinet officer, has been suggested in many places elsewhere in the course of the many studies of the energy question that have been made in the last few years. It is my considered judgment, however, that this would be a great mistake because energy itself is not only one of our most important, complex, multifaceted, and pressing problems but is likely to continue so for at least the balance of this century. Therefore, once we move along to the idea of setting it up as an item warranting a cabinet post assignment, we ought to recognize its critical importance by not mixing it with other responsibilities. We can well leave these to be taken care of by the Department of the Interior, where they are being taken care of now.

### Pages 26 and 62, by FRANKLIN A. LINDSAY

Although there are clear advantages to a single, consolidated department of energy and natural resources, there is also the danger that the new department will emphasize one technology at the expense of others. Steps must be taken to guard against this danger.

### Pages 26 and 65, by JOHN R. COLEMAN

It is all very well to express the pious hope that EPA might maintain status and influence within a cabinet department on energy. But when the pressures mount to let us go on living just about as we have in the past, it is a reasonable guess that environmental concerns will get short shrift.

### Pages 26 and 65, by ELVIS J. STAHR, *with which* LINCOLN GORDON *has asked to be associated*

I must stress that it is of the greatest importance that EPA be "coordinate, not subordinate." This is easy to state, but it may be so difficult to achieve as a practical matter that it had better not be attempted. Human nature being what it is, and the tendency of Presidents to appoint "experts" in key government positions affecting energy being what it is, one can understand the skepticism with which the concept of combining energy and the environment in a single administration is viewed in many quarters. This problem should be carefully thought through and thoroughly debated to see whether proper safeguards for the general public interest can be built into the proposed new legislation. The tardily recognized need to separate the regulatory from the promotional functions of the old AEC is something of an analogy.

### Pages 26 and 30, by JOSEPH L. BLOCK, *with which* LINCOLN GORDON *and* ELVIS J. STAHR *have asked to be associated*

This statement falls far short of meeting its own objective that "conservation should be a full partner in a strategy for bringing supply and demand into better balance." The recommendations on this score seem inadequate and related primarily to emergency conditions. Surely more vigorous, mandatory measures are needed promptly if what we believe is the major industrial power on earth is not to be browbeaten, black-mailed, and perhaps bankrupted by the sheiks of the OPEC countries.

Many such methods of conserving oil supplies have been suggested. One that should be effective and that appears equitable is to require automobile owners to refrain from using their cars one day each week, on a day of their choice, designated by an appropriate sticker. This would encourage the use of public transportation and pool car riding while eliminating some needless automotive travel. No doubt there are other measures, equally worthy of consideration, that would effectively and fairly curtail demand. One or more of these schemes should be adopted without delay.

### Page 26, by JOHN R. COLEMAN

This policy statement ultimately has a tone of "We'll muddle through without too much change in our lives." The extent of the changes needed to respond to worldwide pressures for more conservative and more equi-table use of resources seems to have escaped us. I suspect that there will need to be more drastic steps on the side of restraining U.S. demand than we allow for. I read us as pussyfooting on the hard questions about de-mand ("Consideration should be given to establishing penalty rates for energy consumption in excess of some reasonable standard," page 27, and "In some cases, this may require restricting auto and truck access to por-tions of the central city at certain times of day," page 40), and elephant-stomping on the easy ones ("We recommend that appliances be clearly labeled to show how much energy they consume").

### Page 26, by LINCOLN GORDON, with which JOHN R. COLEMAN, ROBERT R. NATHAN, and ELVIS J. STAHR have asked to be associated

This policy statement is far too weak, in both tone and content, in its recommendations for energy conservation. A much more vigorous conser-vation effort is feasible without radical changes in life-styles or significant adverse impact on levels of employment and output. It is by far the quick-est means of reducing oil imports. It would improve our bargaining pos-ture toward the oil exporters and enhance the prospects for price stabili-zation or reduction instead of further increases. It would reduce pressures on our balance of payments and somewhat moderate the scale of the petrodollar problem.

During the period to 1985, we should aim at an overall energy consumption growth rate of only 2 percent a year instead of the 2.9 percent shown in the table on page 16. That would bring total energy demand in 1985 down to 93 quads, compared with 105 quads in the table, a difference equivalent to a saving of 5.6 million barrels per day of oil. A vigorous conservation policy would offer far greater flexibility of choice among supply options and import levels and would permit more orderly development of long-term supply alternatives to imported oil.

The major potential savings are in transportation, space heating and cooling, and on a longer time scale, electric power conversion, which should have been singled out for priority attention. Specifically, we should have given emphatic support to a substantial ( $.15 to $.20 per gallon) tax on gasoline, with appropriate relief for low-income users, along with the recommended differential tax on higher-fuel-consumption motor vehicles. A gasoline tax is the best means toward President Ford's modest goal of saving 1 million barrels per day in oil imports by the end of 1975, vastly superior to coupon rationing or to import quotas and the probable resulting service station queues. We should also have stated an order of magnitude for the recommended additional subsidies to public transportation.

*Page 26, by* ROBERT R. NATHAN, *with which* LINCOLN GORDON *and* ELVIS J. STAHR *have asked to be associated*

This is one of CED's finest statements. The strong emphasis on conservation and restraining demand is commendable. However, it does not go far enough, especially relative to the grave emergency this country faces even without another embargo. We must speed and broaden and intensify the support for conservation.

We should not just call for a "review of rate structures for electricity and natural gas to ensure that price differences . . . do not encourage inefficient energy use"; we need rate structures that effectively and positively *discourage* inefficient use. Building codes and regulations were designed without any possible concern about our energy crisis and all of them (not just "where necessary") should be reviewed, with the federal government taking the initiative in establishing strict standards wherever it has the authority and encouraging such standards where it can exercise influence without authority. Furthermore, the specific recommendation to subsidize modernized and expanded public transit must be paralleled by tough public measures to reduce the use of private vehicles. The idea of individual meters in multifamily structures is a good one, and it would also be appropriate to have separate meters for each tenant in commercial buildings.

We need to know much more about price elasticities with respect to use of energy resources. Very large increases in gasoline taxes may well curtail utilization, but the taxes will need to be large to be effective. That means substantial countermeasures will be needed to ease the burden on those least able to pay much higher gasoline prices. A steeply graduated tax on cars in relation to gas usage would be more equitable and perhaps more effective, but that is going to take a considerable period of time to become fully effective. It should be started immediately. We need to experiment with various techniques and devices to achieve the most significant and the most sizable curtailment in gasoline use. If other measures do not bite deep enough, rationing should be applied.

Above all, we need to be tough and even unconventional in meeting these difficult challenges. Reductions in imports of oil should be imposed alongside firm and equitable conservation programs.

*Pages 27 and 39, by* THOMAS G. AYERS

This sentence is the single most objectionable item in the whole statement. I regard this as advocating a totally impractical policy. Taking into account that many residences and businesses use several forms of energy, and the extreme difficulty of adapting and policing standards that will fit the changing circumstances of individual families and businesses, I regard this as pretty silly.

*Pages 27 and 39, by* PHILIP SPORN

I am unalterably opposed to establishing penalty rates for energy consumption in excess of some "reasonable" standard. Although energy is important, surely food is of even greater importance. Yet, with the worldwide crisis we have in food, I have not heard of anybody proposing setting up penalties for food consumption in excess of some "reasonable" food standard. Who is to determine what is a reasonable energy standard, and how is it to be determined? If an ill elderly person is confined to bed in a room that is not heated and uses an electric heater to keep from sliding into a deeper illness, are we to deny that person the saving grace of the electric heater? Have we gotten to the point where we have to do that?

*Pages 27 and 39, by* ROBERT D. LILLEY, *with which* LINCOLN GORDON
*and* ELVIS J. STAHR *have asked to be associated*

The promotion of recycling of material should also involve the removal of transportation regulations that discriminate against recycled materials and goods. For example, freight rates for recycled paper are much higher than those for virgin paper.

*Pages 27 and 41, by* OSCAR A. LUNDIN, *with which*
C. WREDE PETERSMEYER *has asked to be associated*

The motor vehicle industry has a large and immediate concern for energy-related issues. Policies in this area impact directly on our day-to-day business operation, and much thought and careful analysis have been directed at determining the proper parameters of a wise future energy program.

Against this background of examination, I cannot concur with the specific recommendation that a higher tax be applied to higher-fuel-consumption motor vehicles.

In the first place, it has long been my view that, in general, the proper function of the tax system is to generate revenue, not to implement social policy. The history of the overall value of special-purpose taxes argues in this direction. They tend to misallocate resources and, over time, outlive any usefulness they once may have had.

In the specific case of a tax on high-energy-consumption motor vehicles, there are even more pointed objections. Vehicle energy consumption is directly related to vehicle weight, and much of that weight is attributable to such desired, and in many cases mandated, vehicle characteristics as safety and performability. For example, the man with a larger family requires a larger car, and heavy commerce requires heavy trucks. To the extent that such requirements can be met with smaller vehicles, there are already sufficient fuel price incentives to cause that to happen. These same forces, acting through the discipline of the competitive process, are also already forcing manufacturers to make maximum effort to reduce weight without sacrificing certain required aspects of vehicle performance.

There is therefore no current need for such a tax. Moreover, if energy price controls are abandoned, as they should be, and all fuel prices seek their proper market clearing levels, the free market allocating mechanism will serve to direct economic activity even more efficiently. This should be greatly preferred to any arbitrary taxing scheme as a method to encourage energy conservation and develop domestic supplies.

If, however, some form of energy consumption tax is adopted as public policy, it should be an evenhanded, nondiscriminatory tax on all undue energy consumption. The concept of social equity would require no less.

*Pages 27 and 41, by* ROBERT B. SEMPLE

With regard to the recommendation to develop a consistent national policy to apply a higher tax to higher-fuel-consumption motor vehicles, I am not against a uniformly applied weight tax in the licensing of automobiles, as is done in most states, but I do not approve of a tax on fuel consumption per se. It just does not appear that this could be done in an equitable manner and that the effects of price in the marketplace would eventually accomplish most of what is desired in the way of conservation in this area.

*Pages 27 and 32, by* ELVIS J. STAHR

I would also recommend major cutbacks in the energy and dollars expended on the interstate high-speed highway construction program.

*Pages 27, 29, 33, and 47, by* THOMAS G. AYERS, *with which* JOHN D. HARPER *has asked to be associated*

In principle, capturing excess profits or windfalls is a great idea. In practice, it is likely to produce more inequities than it cures.

*Pages 27, 29, 33, and 47, by* JOSEPH L. BLOCK, *with which* GILBERT E. JONES *and* C. WREDE PETERSMEYER *have asked to be associated*

I have no objection to capturing so-called "windfall profits" through taxation and heartily commend channeling them "into net additions to energy-producing investment." However, in my judgment, much too much has been said in the press and in Congress about the increased profits of the oil companies and much too little about the imperative need of getting on with the job of remedying the energy shortage. One would think that the culprits are the American oil companies rather than the sheiks, that the latter and not the former discovered, developed, and marketed these much-needed petroleum products.

It is most likely that the concentration on the subject of oil company taxation and its uncertainty has delayed projects and lessened investor interest to the detriment of the ultimate objective of increasing energy supplies as rapidly as possible. And surely Congress and the public need to be reminded repeatedly of the dire need for profits to finance the gigantic exploration and development programs that must be undertaken.

*Pages 27 and 33, by* JAMES R. KENNEDY, *with which* LINCOLN GORDON *has asked to be associated*

I recommend that the wellhead price of *new* natural gas be deregulated and that the demand-reducing effects of higher prices be allowed to function. This deregulation should not be allowed to disrupt or abrogate current contracts.

*Pages 27 and 33, by* ROBERT B. SEMPLE

I consider the suggestion that windfall profit taxes on "old" gas be used to reduce taxes on low-income consumers that burn gas to be a poor concept and virtually impossible to administer. "Old" gas differentials should better be dealt with through the regulative agencies, that is, the Federal Power Commission and the state public service commissions.

*Page 28, by* ROBERT R. NATHAN

Most of this statement's proposed measures for expanding supplies are commendable, especially with respect to actions designed to speed and enlarge exploration and exploitation of new energy sources. Also, all feasible steps must be expedited to increase coal output and transport capacities promptly. This does raise the serious question of common ownership of different sources of energy.

Is it in the national interest for the oil companies to own more and more coal resources? Should and can healthy competition be assured between different fuels? Are very large profits for oil companies the best way to achieve investments in much more coal mining and transport capacity or to increase research and development expenditures for getting oil from shale or to enlarge supplies of synthetic fuel and related sources of energy? The combination of vigorous competition between modes of energy sources and government actions to provide strong developmental incentives would better serve the nation's interests.

Another major policy issue relates to decontrol of oil and gas prices. Under decontrol, the statement properly calls for excess profits taxes to capture windfalls on existing contracts. But what about "new" oil and gas? Also, in view of the serious inflation now raging and the high degree of uncertainty of the supply responses to decontrol of the wellhead price of natural gas and of the price of "old" oil, the proposal is objectionable. In view of the continuing shortages, prices of domestic oil will tend to equal the politically determined import prices. What level of domestic prices is needed to bring increased domestic supply, and how much more supply and for how long? Secondary recovery of oil costs more. But should the price to encourage this higher-cost supply be set only by import prices? What rise will be needed in the natural gas price to find and exploit more gas fields? Should that price be determined by high-cost liquified natural gas or by even higher priced synthetic gas? Other incentives for further exploration may be far more efficient than price decontrol and recapture of excess profits on only "old" oil and gas. Also, if higher prices were desirable for discouraging consumption, excise taxes would appear preferable, with the proceeds assigned to exploration incentives or for offsetting some of the high price of imported oil and gas.

*Pages 28 and 47, by* PHILIP SPORN

This paragraph certainly takes in a lot of territory, and I want to comment on three items.

1. What we need is not more "efficient" controls but more balanced controls. In a very narrow sense, the present controls are too efficient. They throttle the subject of their control.

2. The "streamlining" of procedures for leasing shale deposits may be a good thing, but I do not believe that will contribute much to expediting production of oil from oil shales. In the *Wall Street Journal*, November 14, 1974, John M. Hopkins, vice-president, refining and marketing, Union Oil Company of California, notes that the capital required to produce certain shale oil is estimated at $12,000 to $15,000 per barrel of daily capacity. At a capital charge of 20 percent, this amounts to $2,400 to $3,000 per year. At the latter figure, if you assume a yearly production of 300 barrels per barrel of daily capacity, this amounts to a $10 capital charge per barrel of shale oil for facilities alone, without any allowance for the cost of the shale or the material and labor for the operation and maintenance of the equipment. This is the reason why in opting for a program of conversion of "coal, tar sands, and oil shale" in my comment on page 15, I qualified it by postulating "as technology and economics make feasible."

3. It is not clear whether the purpose of the leasing program recommended is intended to provide for extraction, processing, or conversion. Quite likely, each of the fuel items has a different objective that needs to be clearly spelled out.

*Pages 28 and 47, by* SIDNEY J. WEINBERG, JR., *with which* LINCOLN GORDON *and* C. WREDE PETERSMEYER *have asked to be associated*

We have enormous domestic reserves of coal. The recommendation should place greater emphasis on the role coal must play in resolving our energy problem. A timely and practical energy policy should actively encourage the use of coal as our principal U.S. source of electrical energy. A paragraph on page 45 states the facts, but it needs emphasis here.

*Pages 29 and 47, by* JAMES R. KENNEDY, *with which* LINCOLN GORDON *and* GILBERT E. JONES *have asked to be associated*

I support the deregulation of *new* oil and the classification of oil produced from secondary recovery techniques as *new* oil.

*Pages 29 and 47, by* GEORGE C. McGHEE, *with which* LINCOLN GORDON *has asked to be associated*

Further decontrol of the price of "old" domestic oil should begin now with oil being produced by secondary methods and other high-production-cost oil to prevent premature abandonment of reserves that cannot profitably be produced at present controlled prices. This could then be expanded to include new secondary recovery projects and other production as costs rise. This would also have the effect of cushioning the estimated $9 billion inflationary impact of complete decontrol and eliminate necessity for a "windfall" profits tax on oil that can still be produced at a cost below the present controlled price.

*Pages 29 and 55, by* IAN MacGREGOR, *with which* LINCOLN GORDON, JOHN D. HARPER, GILBERT E. JONES, *and* C. WREDE PETERSMEYER *have asked to be associated*

The recommendation to reduce the "front-end costs of oil and gas leases" fails to mention that the same problem arises with respect to coal leases, where the National Coal Association and the American Mining Congress have both urged that front-end bidding be replaced by systems of royalties on production.

*Pages 29 and 54, by* ELVIS J. STAHR

In addition to the use of solid waste as an energy source, I would suggest the use of wind machines.

*Pages 29 and 54, by* PHILIP SPORN

The research program postulated in this paragraph troubles me deeply. We are living in an age where research is worshiped with a fervor that very few people generate in giving substance to their religious or ethical beliefs. But since we are operating under a Damoclean threat, it is necessary that we moderate our research religiosity and focus it more sharply and more selectively, researching in particular those areas that will help us achieve Project Independence. This will make for a more productive research program and give us results at an earlier date. It will also save us from carrying out a substantial basic research program in solar energy where we need no basic research, in geothermal energy, which needs it even less. With these savings in money and in manpower, it will make possible a more intensive basic program in fusion, where we are carrying out a major program right now, and a more intensive applied research and development program to give us a breeder.

As to international coordination, to postulate international coordination whenever possible is, I believe, a mistake. The entire program should be basically a U.S. program, except that where opportunities present themselves to carry out research and development in cooperation with any foreign nation or nations, this should be taken advantage of, *provided it can be done without introducing additional delays.* We simply cannot jeopardize our future safety or welfare by losing any appreciable time in smoothing the ruffles always generated in widespread international cooperative efforts.

*Pages 29 and 54, by* ELVIS J. STAHR

Bare mention, at least, should also be made of wind energy, the technology for which has long been known, and of ocean-wave energy, which is already being worked on seriously by at least one foreign country. The United States is rather well supplied with both winds and waves.

*Page 38, by* ROBERT D. LILLEY

Subsidies interfere with the operation of a free market and tend to grow unless their area of use is carefully defined. Since nearly everyone will be disadvantaged in some way by the energy problem, a subsidy program could be an endless process unless it is rigidly limited. Because of this tendency, this recommendation seems too general and vague, and the examples on the preceding pages do not offer sufficient additional guidance. Moreover, this statement seems broader than the summary recommendation on the subject on page 28.

*Page 38, by* ROBERT D. LILLEY, *with which* LINCOLN GORDON, ROBERT R. NATHAN, *and* ELVIS J. STAHR *have asked to be associated*

Industry seems capable of greater energy savings than is implied here. Apart from transportation, the assumption seems to be that higher energy costs alone will stimulate energy conservation by industry. Although this is undoubtedly true, the savings of energy can be increased through special programs, even where energy costs may not be major factors in an industry's cost structure. For example, some industries have achieved considerable success in energy conservation, due in part to well-defined energy-conservation programs that include the setting of objectives and the measurement of results. Some such focus on industry conservation programs would be helpful.

*Page 46, by* ELVIS J. STAHR

By no means all the scientific community is optimistic that the safety and safeguard problems inherent in nuclear energy can be completely solved in the immediate future or perhaps ever. For this and other reasons, I believe that crash programs on a scale far greater than presently contemplated in solar energy and possibly geothermal and wind energy should be undertaken without delay. A nuclear program of the size envisaged in the preceding paragraph would cost scores of billions of dollars and would make it almost impossible to turn back, no matter what the risks of going forward. See also my comment regarding page 49.

*Page 48, by* GEORGE C. McGHEE, *with which* ROBERT B. SEMPLE *has asked to be associated*

I do not believe that this offers a practical solution. There is no such thing as absolute safety. Accidents can always occur. The principal experience in this country, however, in offshore drilling, which is presumably the issue under discussion, has occurred in the Gulf of Mexico, where exploration and production from hundreds of wells over decades has resulted in extremely few spills or other environmental threats, none of catastrophic magnitude.

*Page 49, by* ELVIS J. STAHR

I certainly agree that maximum effort should be put into nuclear safety. However, I am seriously concerned about the statement's tendency to equate risks in the nuclear field with risks in other human activities. There is a *qualitative* difference between nuclear systems that are not perfectly safe and transportation systems that are not perfectly safe or wiring and heating apparatus that can cause accidents. That difference is because of something called *radioactivity,* which, unlike the other hazards mentioned, persists for generations, even centuries. I am not talking about the danger of explosion, such as an atomic bomb, but rather of the enormous dangers of plutonium and the not inconsiderable dangers involved in processing, transporting, and storing nuclear material and wastes in general. This, plus the fact that it is not exportable (because it would be even more unsafe in the hands of most other nations), makes the nuclear option unattractive, even if we *can* make it "almost perfectly safe."

The same billions (or some of the billions) of dollars needed to solve these problems (assuming they can be solved) and to construct hundreds of nuclear power plants in the next decade or two could make possible the breakthrough needed for large-scale generation and storage of electricity from solar energy and the widespread application of known technologies for utilizing solar heating and cooling as well as wind, geothermal, and possibly, wave energy. *These* technologies *are* safely exportable to the billions of people in the developing countries, whose energy needs are even more serious than ours.

*Page 53, by* FRANKLIN A. LINDSAY, *with which* LINCOLN GORDON, ROBERT R. NATHAN, *and* ELVIS J. STAHR *have asked to be associated*

Solar energy may be able to make a significant contribution to energy needs in a relatively shorter time than required for some of the other newer sources, provided research and development on the basic technology of both thermal and direct electric conversion is successful. The reason for some optimism is that unlike other sources such as nuclear power and shale refining, huge central facilities, each taking seven to ten years to build, are likely not to be required. Solar energy collectors and converters will be very simple and can come in small modules manufactured in mass production facilities and installed locally. Furthermore, long-distance high-capacity power lines or coal and oil transportation systems would not be required because of installation at or near the user.

The requirement for "dependable" sunlight for effective solar energy conversion may be overstated in this statement. Both light scattered by clouds and direct sunlight can be trapped by collectors designed to heat and cool dwellings. And the sum of direct and scattered light is abundant enough for utilization in almost all parts of the United States. For example, on a yearly basis, Boston receives almost 80 percent as much useful solar energy as Miami does.

### Page 54, by ROBERT D. LILLEY

The increased costs of new electric utility plants that need to be allowed for by rate regulation include higher capital costs as a whole, comprising not only higher interest costs on borrowed capital but also higher costs of equity capital, which is an indispensable element in public utility financing.

### Page 60, by THOMAS G. AYERS

This sentence is to me both inaccurate and gratuitous.

# CED
# A Business-Academic
# Partnership

## Objectives of the Committee for Economic Development

For three decades, the Committee for Economic Development has had a respected influence on business and public policy. Composed of two hundred leading business executives and educators, CED is devoted to these two objectives:

*To develop, through objective research and informed discussion, findings and recommendations for private and public policy which will contribute to preserving and strengthening our free society, achieving steady economic growth at high employment and reasonably stable prices, increasing productivity and living standards, providing greater and more equal opportunity for every citizen, and improving the quality of life for all.*

*To bring about increasing understanding by present and future leaders in business, government, and education and among concerned citizens of the importance of these objectives and the ways in which they can be achieved.*

CED's work is supported strictly by private voluntary contributions from business and industry, foundations, and individuals. It is independent, nonprofit, nonpartisan, and nonpolitical.

The two hundred trustees, who generally are presidents or board chairmen of corporations and presidents of universities, are chosen for their individual capacities rather than as representatives of any particular interests. By working with scholars, they unite business judgment and experience with scholarship in analyzing the issues and developing recommendations to resolve the economic problems that constantly arise in a dynamic and democratic society.

Through this business-academic partnership, CED endeavors to develop policy statements and other research materials that commend themselves as guides to public and business policy; for use as texts in college economics and political science courses and in management training courses; for consideration and discussion by newspaper and magazine editors, columnists, and commentators; and for distribution abroad to promote better understanding of the American economic system.

CED believes that by enabling businessmen to demonstrate constructively their concern for the general welfare, it is helping business to earn and maintain the national and community respect essential to the successful functioning of the free enterprise capitalist system.

## Statements on National Policy
## Issued by the Research
## and Policy Committee
*(publications in print)*

---

Achieving Energy Independence *(December 1974)*

A New U.S. Farm Policy for Changing World Food Needs *(October 1974)*

Congressional Decision Making for National Security *(September 1974)*

*Toward a New International Economic System:
   A Joint Japanese-American View *(June 1974)*

More Effective Programs for a Cleaner Environment *(April 1974)*

The Management and Financing of Colleges *(October 1973)*

Strengthening the World Monetary System *(July 1973)*

Financing the Nation's Housing Needs *(April 1973)*

Building a National Health-Care System *(April 1973)*

*A New Trade Policy Toward Communist Countries *(September 1972)*

High Employment Without Inflation:
   A Positive Program for Economic Stabilization *(July 1972)*

Reducing Crime and Assuring Justice *(June 1972)*

Military Manpower and National Security *(February 1972)*

The United States and the European Community *(November 1971)*

Improving Federal Program Performance *(September 1971)*

Social Responsibilities of Business Corporations *(June 1971)*

Education for the Urban Disadvantaged:
   From Preschool to Employment *(March 1971)*

---

*Statements issued in association with CED counterpart organizations in foreign countries.*

Further Weapons Against Inflation *(November 1970)*

Making Congress More Effective *(September 1970)*

*Development Assistance to Southeast Asia *(July 1970)*

Training and Jobs for the Urban Poor *(July 1970)*

Improving the Public Welfare System *(April 1970)*

Reshaping Government in Metropolitan Areas *(February 1970)*

Economic Growth in the United States *(October 1969)*

Assisting Development in Low-Income Countries *(September 1969)*

*Nontariff Distortions of Trade *(September 1969)*

Fiscal and Monetary Policies for Steady Economic Growth *(January 1969)*

Financing a Better Election System *(December 1968)*

Innovation in Education: New Directions for the American School *(July 1968)*

Modernizing State Government *(July 1967)*

*Trade Policy Toward Low-Income Countries *(June 1967)*

How Low Income Countries Can Advance Their Own Growth *(September 1966)*

Modernizing Local Government *(July 1966)*

A Better Balance in Federal Taxes on Business *(April 1966)*

Budgeting for National Objectives *(January 1966)*

Presidential Succession and Inability *(January 1965)*

Educating Tomorrow's Managers *(October 1964)*

Improving Executive Management in the Federal Government *(July 1964)*

Trade Negotiations for a Better Free World Economy *(May 1964)*

Union Powers and Union Functions: Toward a Better Balance *(March 1964)*

Japan in the Free World Economy *(April 1963)*

Economic Literacy for Americans *(March 1962)*

Cooperation for Progress in Latin America *(April 1961)*

---

*Statements issued in association with CED counterpart organizations in foreign countries.*

7200-4
5-09
C
B-T

## CED Counterpart Organizations in Foreign Countries

Close relationships exist between the Committee for Economic Development and independent, nonpolitical research organizations in other countries. Such counterpart groups are composed of business executives and scholars and have objectives similar to those of CED, which they pursue by similarly objective methods. CED cooperates with these organizations on research and study projects of common interest to the various countries concerned. This program has resulted in a number of joint policy statements involving such international matters as East-West trade, assistance to the developing countries, and the reduction of nontariff barriers to trade.

---

**CEDA**    Committee for Economic Development of Australia
*128 Exhibition Street, Melbourne, Victoria, Australia*

**CEPES**   Europäische Vereinigung für
Wirtschaftliche und Soziale Entwicklung
*56 Friedrichstrasse, Dusseldorf, West Germany*

**PEP**    Political and Economic Planning
*12 Upper Belgrave Street, London, SWIX 8BB, England*

**経済同友会**    Keizai Doyukai
(Japan Committee for Economic Development)
*Japan Industrial Club Bldg.*
*1 Marunouchi, Chiyoda-ku, Tokyo, Japan*

**CRC**    Centre de Recherches et d'Etudes des Chefs d'Entreprise
*31 Avenue Pierre 1$^{er}$ de Serbie, Paris (16$^{eme}$), France*

**SNS**    Studieförbundet Näringsliv och Samhälle
*Sköldungagatan, 2, 11427 Stockholm, Sweden*

Stories of

# Mummies

## and the Living Dead

Eric Kudalis

Capstone Press

MINNEAPOLIS

Printed in the United States of America.

Capstone Press • 2440 Fernbrook Lane • Minneapolis, MN  55447

Editorial Director     John Coughlan
Managing Editor     John Martin
Copy Editor     Theresa Early
Editorial Assistant     Michelle Wood

*Library of Congress Cataloging-in-Publication Data*

Kudalis, Eric, 1960-
     Stories of mummies and the living dead / Eric Kudalis.
          p.  cm. -- (Classic monster stories)
     Includes bibliographical references and index.
     Summary:  When its casket is opened, an Egyptian mummy comes to life and tries to raise a princess from the dead.  Includes information about other mummy stories and about how mummies were made in Egypt.
     ISBN  1-56065-214-4 (lib. bdg.)
     [1. Mummies--Fiction.  2. Mummies.]  I. Title.
     II. Series.
PZ7.K94855St   1994
[Fic]--dc20                                        93-42832
                                                        CIP
                                                         AC

ISBN: 1-56065-214-4
99 98 97 96 95 94          8 7 6 5 4 3 2 1

# Table of Contents

Chapter 1   The Best-Known Mummy Story....... 5

Chapter 2   Other Mummy Stories ................... 27

Chapter 3   What Is a Mummy?........................ 29

Chapter 4   Ancient Egypt and Its Mummies .... 31

Chapter 5   How to Make a Mummy ................. 37

Chapter 6   Modern Scientists Look
              at a Mummy ................................. 41

Glossary ........................................... 44

To Learn More ................................... 46

Index ................................................ 47

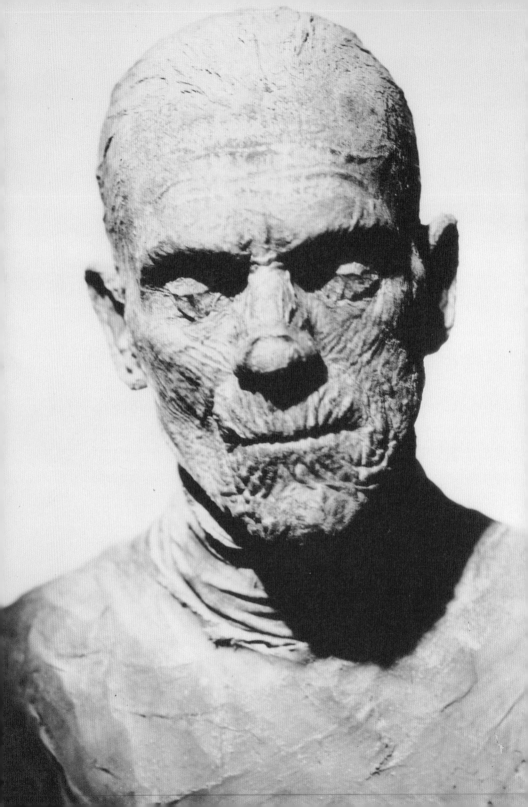

# Chapter 1

# The Best-Known Mummy Story

Almost everyone is fascinated by mummies. There are many legends and stories about these ancient, **preserved** bodies. One of the best known is told in a 1932 movie called *The Mummy*.

## The Story of *The Mummy*

The hot wind blew sand across the **excavation** site. Professor Muller, Sir Joseph Whemple, and Ralph Norton stood by the ancient grave.

They came from the British Museum Field Expedition to dig up Im-ho-tep, a 3,700-year-old Egyptian mummy.

The three men pried open the coffin. Inside, the mummy lay wrapped in decayed bandages.

"Look. His head is turned to one side," Professor Muller said. "It looks as though he was buried alive."

They explored the site for clues. Norton noticed a small golden box shaped like a **casket**.

## Egyptian Curse in a Box

Sir Joseph read the Egyptian **inscription**: "Death to anyone who opens this casket."

Ralph Norton laughed. "Nonsense. Let's open it and see what's inside."

"No, don't," Muller warned. "It could be dangerous."

Sir Joseph insisted. "Perhaps it contains a clue to Im-ho-tep's death."

"Let's keep the box until morning and then decide what to do with it," Muller said.

## Inside the Box

That night in the field laboratory, Norton worked alone. Near him lay the casket of Im-ho-tep.

Norton couldn't keep his mind on his work. "I owe it to science to look inside the box," he thought.

He lifted the box onto his worktable and opened the lid. Inside was a **brittle scroll**. He unrolled it and read the words.

It was the Scroll of Thoth, a spell to raise the dead. The goddess Isis, according to the legend, used the spell to raise her husband, Osiris, from the dead.

Norton thought he heard a noise behind him. He turned but there was nothing.

He went back to reading.

"…We live today. We shall live again."

He heard footsteps. He turned. The mummy of Im-ho-tep stood above him.

## The Mummy

With torn bandages dangling from his arms, the mummy reached out. Norton screamed and fell backward.

The mummy grabbed the scroll and lurched out the door. Norton's screams grew louder. He laughed **hysterically**.

Sir Joseph and Professor Muller ran into the room and found Norton in the corner.

"You should have seen his face," he said.

Muller and Sir Joseph saw that the mummy was gone. It was stolen, no doubt, but they couldn't explain Norton's behavior.

Still Norton laughed. It was the laugh of an insane man.

## The Search for Another Mummy

Eleven years later, Sir Joseph Whemple's son, Frank, was at a dusty excavation site. Frank was an **archaeologist**. His father ran the Cairo Museum.

**The mummy lives!**

 Frank was looking for the mummy of
Princess Anck-es-en-Amon. So far all he had
found was some pottery.

Frank was in his laboratory. He heard a knock at the door. A tall man stood in the doorway. His face was very wrinkled.

"I am Ardath Bey," the man said. "I know where Anck-es-en-Amon's grave is. Follow me."

## To the Site of the Mummy

Ardath Bey led Frank and his men to an unknown place. After several days of digging, the archaeologists found a casket.

"We've found it!" Frank screamed. When he turned to thank the stranger, Ardath Bey was gone.

Newspapers ran stories of the discovery. The mummy was displayed at the Cairo Museum.

Ardath Bey had disappeared, but he followed the newspaper accounts closely.

One day he went to the museum. He hid until the museum closed. Then he went to Anck-es-en-Amon.

**Ardath Bey leads the men to the location of the mummy's tomb.**

Ardath Bey knelt beside the tomb and unrolled the Scroll of Thoth. He began to read the spell.

## A Mysterious Voice
Helen Grosvenor was Professor Muller's houseguest. She was at a party.

Helen kept hearing a distant voice. She thought someone was calling out to her.

At the museum, Ardath Bey continued to read his chant.

Helen fell into a **trance**. She walked out the door and got into a taxi. The taxi drove across town to the Cairo Museum.

She pounded on the locked doors of the museum.

"Im-ho-tep!" she called.

## Ardath Bey's Escape

Frank and Sir Joseph were on their way home from the museum when they saw Helen. They hurried toward her.

Helen fainted.

Inside, a guard discovered Ardath Bey praying beside the mummy.

"The museum is closed," he warned.

Ardath Bey grabbed the guard by the neck and shook him violently. The guard fell to the floor dead.

Ardath Bey ran from the museum without the scroll.

## Speaking in Ancient Egyptian

Meanwhile, Frank and Sir Joseph took Helen to their house. She seemed to be in a deep trance. She began to mutter something.

"She's speaking some foreign language," Sir Joseph said. "I think it's ancient Egyptian — which hasn't been spoken in 3,000 years."

They sent for Dr. Muller. As the three men puzzled over Helen's condition, an inspector came to the Whemples' house with the scroll and told them about the murder.

Sir Joseph and Muller had never seen the scroll before. Sir Joseph said that he had often seen Ardath Bey near the mummy of Anck-es-en-Amon.

## The Mummy Rose from the Dead

"Strange, isn't it?" Muller said. "Ardath Bey seems to have appeared from nowhere. Yet he knew where to find Anck-es-en-Amon. This scroll is used to raise the dead. Ten years ago, the mummy of Im-ho-tep disappeared, and with it the forbidden box."

"What are you getting at?" Sir Joseph asked.

"The mummy was not stolen," Muller said. "The mummy rose from the dead when Norton read the scroll. Ardath Bey is the mummy. Now he wants to raise the Princess Anck-es-en-Amon from the dead."

"Come on, Muller. Just because someone visits a museum doesn't mean he's a living mummy," Sir Joseph said.

Suddenly they heard Helen speaking in the next room.

### "You are Anck-es-en-Amon."

The men went to the door. Ardath Bey was there. His eyes were fixed on Helen.

"I know you from before," he said to Helen.

"That's impossible," Helen said.

"In Thebes, long ago, we loved each other," Ardath Bey said. "But the gods took you away from me. Now I've found you again. You are

Anck-es-en-Amon, living in the body of Helen Grosvenor."

Sir Joseph turned to Frank and said, "Take Helen home."

## Struggle for the Scroll

When Frank left with Helen, Muller said to Ardath Bey, "We know you are the mummy Im-ho-tep. What do you want from us?"

"I've come for the scroll," Ardath Bey said.

Sir Joseph refused to give it to him. Ardath Bey stretched out his hand. A ring on his finger sent out a bright light that knocked Sir Joseph to the ground.

Muller grabbed the scroll. He held it over the fireplace. "I'll burn the scroll if you don't leave."

"I'll go," Ardath Bey said. "But I will be back."

## A Plot of Revenge

Ardath Bey plotted his revenge. In his home he knelt before a pool of water.

**Ardath Bey**

The water swirled.  Soon an image of Sir Joseph appeared.  Suddenly he grabbed his chest.  He gasped as he fell to his death.

Now Ardath Bey would get his scroll.
Ardath Bey cast a spell on a servant so that the
man would get the scroll for him.

## Strange Wandering

Helen could not forget Ardath Bey. One
morning she left Muller's house. She
wandered through Cairo. She felt something
calling her.

Finally she arrived at a large house.

Ardath Bey came toward her.

"Welcome," he said. "I knew you would come."

## Helen's Past

Ardath Bey said, "For thousands of years
we've been separated."

He crouched next to the pool. Helen was in
a trance.

"Look in the reflecting pool and you will see
your past," Ardath Bey said.

In the pool Helen saw images of her other
lives. She was a princess, a Viking woman,
and a French noblewoman. Finally, she saw
herself 3,700 years back in Egypt.

**Ardath Bey explains the past to Helen.**

She was Princess Anck-es-en-Amon, the daughter of the **Pharaoh** Amenophis, a priestess of the Goddess Isis.

"I was Im-ho-tep, the high priest of the Temple of the Sun," Ardath Bey said. "I loved you more than any man ever loved a woman. But you grew sick and died."

Anck-es-en-Amon was mummified and buried.

## Buried Alive

"I could not live without you," Ardath Bey continued. "I stole the Scroll of Thoth from the statue Osiris."

Im-ho-tep had sneaked into the **crypt**. He lifted Anck-es-en-Amon from her stone coffin and read from the scroll.

"Rise from the dead!" he had cried.

The pharaoh's guards had burst into the crypt. They dragged Im-ho-tep to prison.

"You have committed a crime against the gods by stealing the scroll," the Pharaoh said. "For this you will be buried alive."

The soldiers wrapped him in mummy's bandages. They then lowered Im-ho-tep's coffin into the crypt, along with the Scroll of Thoth.

## "Such Strange Dreams"

Helen woke with a jerk.

"Have I been asleep?" she asked. "I had

such strange dreams. I dreamed I was a princess in ancient Egypt."

Satisfied that he had shown Helen her past, Ardath Bey let her leave. Helen wandered home. She couldn't remember where she had been.

"We will watch her closely," Muller said. "No doubt Im-ho-tep will call her again."

Helen slept badly that night. She heard Im-ho-tep calling her. She rose and sneaked out. At the museum, the servant opened the door and Helen entered.

## "You Must Die So You Can Rise Again"

Im-ho-tep stood beside the mummy of Anck-es-en-Amon. He was dressed in his robes of ancient Egypt.

"This mummy is you, and you are the mummy," Im-ho-tep told Helen. "But I cannot raise the mummy, because its soul lives in you. You must die so you can rise again."

Helen wanted to run, but she couldn't.

Im-ho-tep is buried alive.

"I know I was the princess Anck-es-en-Amon," she said. "I loved you once, but now you belong with the dead. I am someone else now. I am young. I want to live."

"I was buried alive for your sake!" he cried. He raised a knife.

Helen ran. She bowed before the statue of Isis and pleaded, "O, Isis, save me."

Isis heard Helen's plea. She raised her arm, and held out a cross-shaped **amulet**.

**Im-ho-tep dressed in his robes of Egypt**

## Free of the Mummy's Curse

Im-ho-tep grabbed Helen. Just as he was about to plunge the knife into her, a burning ray reflected from Isis's amulet and struck Im-ho-tep.

The doomed mummy crumbled to dust. Now Helen was free of the mummy's curse.

Nearly 4,000 years before, Im-ho-tep had offended the gods. Now, as a pile of dust, he received his final punishment.

*The Mummy's Curse* (1945) featured an evil mummy named Kharis.

## *Chapter 2*

# Other Mummy Stories

The success of *The Mummy* led to a series
of mummy movies featuring an evil mummy
called Kharis.  The first was *The Mummy's
Hand* in 1940.  Like Im-ho-tep in *The Mummy,*
Kharis was buried alive for offending the gods.

Other movies featuring Kharis are *The
Mummy's Tomb* (1942), *The Mummy's Ghost*
(1944), and *The Mummy's Curse* (1945).

Hammer Studios in England had success in
remaking such classic movies as *Frankenstein*
and *Dracula*.  In 1959 the film company
launched a series of movies, beginning with
*The Mummy.*   It starred Christopher Lee and
Peter Cushing.

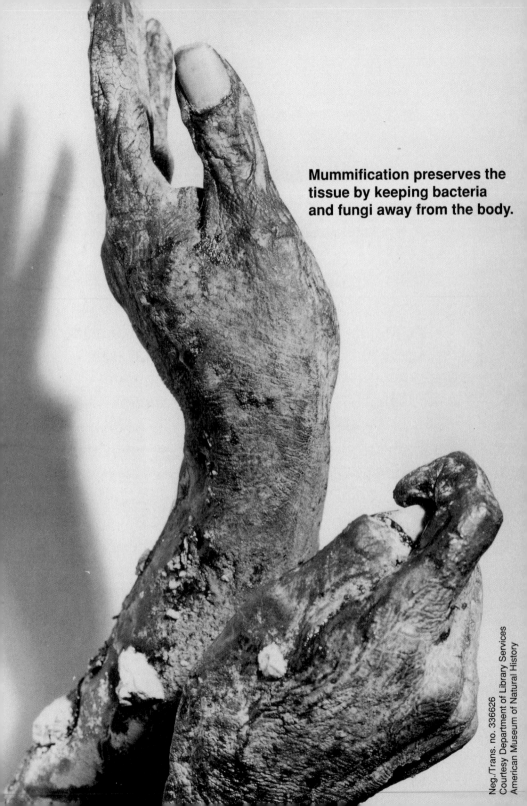

**Mummification preserves the tissue by keeping bacteria and fungi away from the body.**

# Chapter 3

# What Is a Mummy?

A mummy is the preserved body of a human or animal. Mummies are found throughout the world in Egypt, Europe, Asia, North America, and South America.

A dead body may be preserved by accident or on purpose. Mummification keeps **bacteria** and **fungi** from destroying the dead body's tissues, such as the skin. A body may be mummified when it is dried out quickly by chemicals, smoke, or fire. A body left to dry in the hot desert air will also become a mummy.

Sealing a body in an airtight container will mummify it. Mummies have also been found frozen in glaciers, buried in marshy bogs, and sealed in caves.

# Chapter 4

# Ancient Egypt and Its Mummies

The most famous mummies are from Egypt. Egyptians began mummifying their dead nearly 5,000 years ago. They tried many methods for **embalming** a **corpse**.

At first, only Egyptian rulers, the pharaohs, were mummified. In time, the pharaohs' wives, children, relatives, officials, priests, and servants were also mummified. They were supposed to join the pharaohs in the afterlife.

Soon, most wealthy Egyptians arranged for their mummification after death. Archaeologists estimate the Egyptians created mummies for 3,000 years.

## Life after Death

Egyptians made mummies because they believed in an afterlife. The Egyptians believed that the spirit of a dead person would stay in the tomb to be close to its body. The body needed to be preserved to give the spirit a place to rest. Magic spells were said over the mummy to turn it into an **immortal** being.

## Tombs and Pyramids

Tombs were considered houses for the dead. Tombs had everything the dead would need to make their afterlife comfortable. Food, clothing, books, medicine, gold, jewels, weapons, and furniture were buried with the dead.

More than 70 pharaohs built pyramids above their tombs. The most famous are the three great pyramids at Giza. They were built more than 4,500 years ago for the pharaohs Cheops, Chephren, and Mycerinus.

**The three great pyramids at Giza**

One of the most important archaeological finds of the 20th century was the discovery of the tomb of Tutankhamen. He was a pharaoh, or king, who reigned nearly 3,358 years ago during the 18th Dynasty.

Tutankhamen's tomb was a golden splendor of ornament. Objects included furniture, clothing, jewels, masks, weapons, and more.

The burial chamber above Tutankhamen's **sarcophagus** is painted with scenes of the journey from the world of the living to the

world of the dead. Egyptians stopped
mummifying around A.D. 300.

Universal Studios' *The Mummy*

## Chapter 5

# How to Make a Mummy

For the Egyptians, embalming had an important religious meaning. The holy man in charge was called the "Controller of the Mysteries." He had several assistants. Embalming took several steps. The whole process took 70 days.

### Removing the Internal Organs

First the embalmers washed the dead body. Using a long hook, they pulled the brain out through the nose. Then they made a cut in the

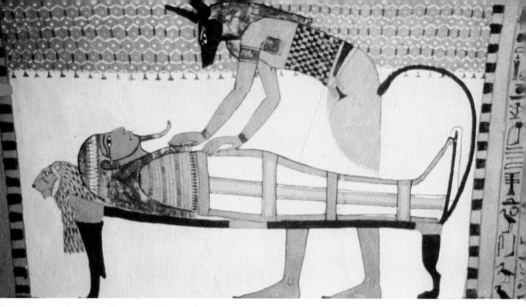

**According to Egyptian legend, Anubis, who had a jackal's head, is the god of embalming**

side of the body and took out the lungs, stomach, liver, and intestines.

The heart was important. The Egyptians believed it held the mind. The embalmers wrapped up the heart and left it inside the chest. They put the other organs in special pots.

## Drying the Body

The body was washed inside and out with wine. The embalmers then stuffed the body with cotton and laid it on a bed of salt. The salt drew water from the body. The body was left to dry for about 40 days.

When the body was dried, the cloth inside was replaced with new stuffing—cloth, mud, sawdust, or other materials. Embalmers rubbed the skin of the corpse with perfume and oils. They poured warm resin over it, to form a protective seal. Then the body was decorated with jewelry and makeup.

## The Wrapping

Next was the important task of wrapping the mummy in layers and layers of linen bandages. Each finger, toe, arm, and leg was wrapped. The holy man took special care with the head.

Jewels and charms were placed on top of the cloth. The workers poured melted **resin** over every layer of cloth and jewels. The resin made it all stick together.

The wrapping took 15 days. The family and friends of the dead person said many prayers during this time.

Finally, the mummy was laid in a coffin. Sometimes a gold mask was placed over the face. The coffin might be put inside several other brightly decorated coffins.

The mummy was ready for burial.

The mummy of Lady Teshat

## Chapter 6

# Modern Scientists Look at a Mummy

Mummies can tell us a lot about ancient Egypt. Scientists study mummies to find out how people lived, what they ate, what diseases they got, and how they died. They even study mummies without unwrapping the bandages.

### A Mysterious Discovery

In 1916 an art museum in Minnesota got a new mummy. The mummy, Lady Teshat, had been a rich Egyptian girl who had lived 3,000 years ago. She had died in her teens.

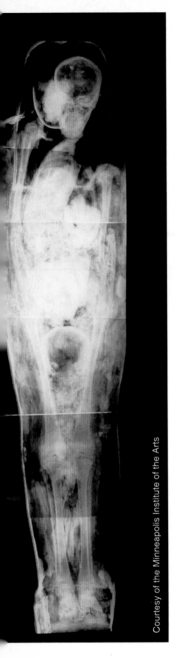

Courtesy of the Minneapolis Institute of the Arts

In 1975, researchers took X rays of the mummy. These pictures showed that the mummy was badly damaged. And there was something very strange–a second skull was resting between the girl's legs!

The amazed scientists didn't know how the skull got there. In 1983, they used a new research tool to try to figure it out. They made a **CT scan** of the mummy.

The scan showed that the mummy had been unwrapped and rewrapped hundreds of years earlier. Researchers guessed that grave robbers looking for jewels had damaged the body and put the skull into the coffin.

Some questions are still unanswered. Whose skull is wrapped up with Lady Teshat? Perhaps new research tools will help solve the mystery someday.

# Glossary

**amulet**–a charm or jewel often believed to have magic power

**archaeologist**–someone who studies people and the way they lived a very long time ago, by looking at the places they lived, worked, and buried their dead

**bacteria**–very simple animals, too small to be seen with the eye

**brittle**–very easily broken

**casket**–coffin or box for burial

**corpse**–dead body

**crypt**–burial room

**CT scan**–computerized picture of the inside of a body (or a mummy)

**embalming**–preparing a corpse for burial with special chemicals and methods to keep it from rotting

**excavation**–a careful, scientific dig to find information about the past

**fungi**–simple plants like molds, yeasts, and mushrooms

**hysterically**–with no control; in a crazy fashion

**immortal**–living forever

**inscription**–words written or carved on something

**pharaoh**–ruler of Egypt, believed by the Egyptians to be a god

**preserved**–kept from rotting

**resin**–a sticky, glue-like stuff, usually made of plant sap

**sarcophagus**–fancy, decorated box to hold a coffin

**scroll**–a roll of paper or leather used for writing upon

**trance**–a state of being unaware of one's surroundings or events; being focused only on something other than the world nearby

# To Learn More

## About mummy movies:

Cohen, Daniel. *Masters of Horror.* New York: Clarion Books, 1984.

Thorne, Ian. *The Mummy.* Mankato, MN: Crestwood House, 1981.

## About mummies:

Putnam, James. *Mummy.* New York: Alfred A. Knopf, 1993.

Reeves, Nicholas. *Into the Mummy's Tomb: The Real-Life Discovery of Tutankhamen's Treasures.* New York: Scholastic, 1992.

Wilcox, Charlotte. *Mummies and Their Mysteries.* Minneapolis: Carolrhoda Books, 1993.

## About ancient Egypt:

Cross, Wilbur. *Egypt.* Chicago: Childrens Press, 1990.

Diamond, Arthur. *Egypt, Gift of the Nile.* New York: Dillon Press, 1992.

Thomsen, Steve. *The Great Pyramid of Cheops.* Mankato, MN: Capstone Press, 1991.

# Index

Anck-es-en-Amon, 10-12, 14-25
Asia, 29

bandages, 7, 9, 20
Bey, Ardath, 10-25

Cairo Museum, 10, 12, 13, 14, 21
casket, 7, 9, 12, 15
Cheops, 33
Chephren, 33
Controller of the Mysteries, 37
CT scan, 42
Cushing, Peter, 27

Dracula, 27
drying the body, 37-38

Egypt, 6, 7, 21, 29, 41
Egyptian beliefs, 31, 32-33, 37, 38; language, 7, 15; mummies, 31-35, 37-39
embalming, 31, 38-39

Europe, 29
Frankenstein, 27

Giza, Egypt, 32
grave robbers, 42
Grosvenor, Helen, 12-25

Im-ho-tep, 6, 7, 9-10, 15, 17, 20-25
Isis, 9, 19, 24-25

jewels, 32-35, 38, 39, 42

Kharis, 27

Lady Teshat, 41-42
Lee, Christopher, 27

Minnesota, 41
Muller, Professor, 5, 7, 10, 12, 15-17, 21
mummies, 29; Egyptian, 31-35, 37-39; preparing the body, 37-39

*Mummy, The* (1932 movie), 5-25, 27; (1959 movie), 27
*Mummy's Curse*, The, 27
*Mummy's Ghost*, The, 27
*Mummy's Hand*, The, 27
*Mummy's Tomb*, The, 27
Mycerinus, 33

North America, 29
Norton, Ralph, 5, 7-10

organs, 37-38
Osiris, 9, 20

pharaoh, 31, 33-35
Pharaoh Amenophis, 19
pyramids, 32-33

resin, 38, 39

Scroll of Thoth, 9, 10, 12, 14, 15, 17, 18, 20-21
South America, 29
spell to raise the dead, 9, 12-14, 15

Temple of the Sun, 20
tomb, 32-35
Tutankhamen, 33-35

Whemple, Frank, 10-12, 14-17
Whemple, Sir Joseph, 5, 7, 10, 14-17
wrappings, 7, 20, 38-39, 41, 42

X rays, 41

*Photo Credits:*
Hollywood Book and Poster: cover, pp. 4, 8, 10, 12, 17, 19, 22-23, 24, 36; Archive Photos: pp. 26, 35; American Museum of Natural History: p. 28; Denver Museum of Natural History: p. 30; Minneapolis Institute of the Arts: pp. 40, 42, 43; Egyptian Tourist Authority: pp. 33, 34-35, 38.